Creative Kids

Party Time

Written by Ina Massler Levin, M.A. and
Michael H. Levin, M.A.

Illustrations by Sue Fullam

Teacher Created Materials

Teacher Created Materials, Inc.

6421 Industry Way

Westminster, CA 92683

www.teachercreated.com

©2000 Teacher Created Materials, Inc.

Made in U.S.A.

ISBN #1-57690-510-1

Library of Congress Catalog Card Number: 99-62481

Editor: Janet Cain
Cover Art: Cheri Macoubrie Wilson

Table of Contents

Table of Contents *(cont,)*

Introduction

A special time is about to arrive for your family. Very soon it will be your child's birthday or a special holiday, and you and your family will want to celebrate. If, when you were a child, you had birthday or holiday parties, you may recall some of the positive feelings associated with these events. It was a time when you got to be the host and have friends over. You may have chosen the food that was served and helped to select the party favors. As an adult, however, you are the organizer and party giver. As your child's party draws near and everyone is getting excited about it, you are starting to feel a bit unsure about what you're going to do. It feels as if you have a hundred questions before you can even begin.

- When and where will we have the party?

- Who will we invite?

- What will we do that's fun and will keep little ones occupied for more than a few minutes?

- How will we be able to afford this party?

These are just some of the questions that you may ask yourself!

The first thing to do is to take a deep breath, sit in a comfortable chair, and read this book. *Party Time* provides you with step-by-step directions for giving a party for your child. Let this book be your guide to planning a party, from what type of invitations to make to writing the thank-you notes. There are even hints for cleaning up along the way so you won't be left with a huge mess at the end of the big event!

Parties should be fun-filled events for both the guests and the hosts. All they take is some organization and a bit of time to plan. Many parties are relatively inexpensive to give. Involving the birthday child makes planning more fun. When everything is prepared before the guests arrive, all you have to do during the party is enjoy watching the children participate in the festivities you have planned for them.

How to Use This Book

This book is designed for you to use as a guide for giving a party for children ages three through eight. It is divided into two sections. The first is a party planner. The second contains themes and ideas for various parties. Throughout the book there are pages that can be reproduced. Some of these are organizational forms that you can fill out when planning a party.

Decide with your birthday child just what type of party to have. Ask your child: Do you want a party where everyone comes dressed up, or would you rather be playing outdoors? Do you want a party where lunch is served or just cake and ice cream? What type of activities do you want to play?

Look at the table of contents and then look through the book. Create a fabulous party featuring your child as the guest of honor by combining any of the ideas from this book that your child likes. Once you have decided on the type of party or the parts of various parties you want to put together, you will need to organize the party. Specific directions for doing this are given on pages 8–90. Make sure to give yourself plenty of time to prepare for the party.

If you are new to giving parties, make it easy on yourself. After reading this book, choose things that you think will be quick and simple for you to do. Most of the activities will fall into that category, but be sure to choose only those that you think you and your child will enjoy. Keep in mind that there is no reason why you cannot combine ideas from the different types of parties suggested in this book.

Use a copier to reproduce the clip art pages. Enlarge or reduce them as needed. You can also scan them into a computer. Then you can use the clip art for decorations, activities, invitations, and thank-you notes.

A Guide for Giving Any Type of Birthday Party

Invitations

Who to Invite

Your child should decide — with your input, of course — who to invite to the party. Before making the guest list, tell your child what a reasonable number of guests is. If your child attends school and you are inviting some of the students in the class but not others, do not have your child distribute the invitations at school. Think of how hurt the children who are not invited will feel when those who are announce that they got invitations. It is far better to get addresses and mail the invitations.

What to Include

Invitations have to include enough information so that the recipients aren't asking questions. The following is standard information for any party invitation.

- Name — Tell the person or group for whom the party is being given.

- Occasion — Indicate the purpose for the party such as a birthday, a summer get-together, or a special celebration.

- Place — Include the street address and the city for the location of the party. This is especially important if someone needs to locate the address on a map.

- Date/Time — Include the date, as well as the starting and ending times. This allows parents to plan their day accordingly.

- Host/Hostess — Tell who is giving the party.

- R.S.V.P. (répondez si'l vous plait) — If you want people to let you know if they are coming, include the name and phone number of a contact person. If you only need to know who isn't coming, write "Regrets Only" under the phone number.

- Phone Number — Even if people don't need to R.S.V.P, include the name and phone number of a contact person. You can write "For Additional Information" under the phone number. Then parents can call if they have questions.

- Optional Information — A map may be included. In addition, provide any special information that parents need to know, such as a particular type of clothing children will need or specific drop-off/pick-up arrangements. You may need to mention if parents are invited to stay with their children. Also, you can ask parents about any food allergies or other things of which you should be aware.

Invitations (cont.)

Types of Invitations

The excitement about attending a party is created the moment the guests receive the invitations. There are many different ways to invite your guests. Depending on the type of party and the amount of time you have to prepare, choose one of the ideas suggested below and on pages 10–13 to begin the party-planning process. Patterns for Four-Fold Invitations and Tri-Fold Invitations are provided on pages 16 and 17.

Telephone Invitations

If you are short on time, the telephone provides a dandy way to contact guests. Not only does it allow you to speak to the person who needs to be the decision-maker regarding attendance, but it also allows you to personalize the invitation. Sometimes you'll know immediately if the invitee can attend.

Use the Party Roster on page 15 for keeping track of telephone invitations. Before calling, make sure you have the correct phone number and the name of the person to whom you should speak. If you are calling parents you do not know, it is best to get their names and ask for Mr. or Mrs. Jones or Becky or Sean Jones. When someone answers the phone, make sure you identify yourself by first and last name and tell who your child is. You may also want to mention how the children know each other. This will help parents know that you are not a salesperson!

It is helpful if you have all the information written out before you begin making the phone calls. An example of what to say for a telephone invitation is provided on the next page.

Telephone Invitations *(cont.)*

Hi, Mrs. Jones, this is Lucy Johnson. I'm Carla's mother. Carla and your daughter Jenna are in the same dance class.

Allow the parent to respond. Then continue by saying:

We're having a party for Carla's sixth birthday at our home on Saturday the 17th from 2 to 4 in the afternoon. It's going to be casual. We're serving ice cream and cake. We hope that Jenna will be able to join us.

Allow the parent to respond. If the parent cannot tell you whether her/his child can attend, continue by saying:

If you can let me know by Wednesday, that would be great. Our phone number is 555-9988.

If the parent says her/his child can attend, continue by saying:

Great! Our address is 8406 Lexington Road, and our phone number is 555-9988. Please feel free to call me if you have any questions. We'll look forward to seeing Jenna on the 17th.

You may want to add more information or talk to the parent a bit longer. However, get to the invitation rather quickly. Make sure you provide all pertinent information, including anything special that the guest might need to bring, such as a bathing suit and towel if you have a swimming activity planned.

Guest Parent(s)	Phone Number	Can Attend	Cannot Attend	Thank-you Note
Nancy Mary Baker	555-1000			
Joel	555-2000			
Mr & Mrs. Jones	555-3000			
Alison	555-4000			

Invitations *(cont.)*

Computer-Generated Invitations

If you have a computer, you can use it to create an invitation. The simplest way is to use a word-processing program. You can add all the pertinent information and center it on the page. If you have access to any of the computer software programs that create cards, they are also a terrific way to make an invitation. These programs generally give you lots of choices. They may include templates and clip art. Just remember to include all the important information on the invitation. If your computer has the capability, you can add clip art or a border. Or better still, let your child draw on the invitation to decorate it. Rubber stamps are also an easy way for children to help liven up their invitations.

Before reproducing the invitation, you can choose some of the special computer papers that are available or make copies on colorful paper. Color ink may also be an option if you have a color printer. Depending on the number of invitations you need, you may wish to print them from your computer printer or have them reproduced at a copy store.

An inexpensive way to perk up invitations is to add stickers to them. This is also a good way to get children involved in creating their party invitations. Most children love adding stickers to just about anything. Why not let your child help you decide which stickers to add? If you have a chosen theme, you might be able to find stickers that go along with that theme.

Invitations that are the size of standard paper can be folded into thirds (page 17). Then you can either put them into legal-sized envelopes or staple and address them so envelopes are not necessary.

Commercial Invitations

There are many wonderful commercially made invitations available. You may wish to purchase some of these. Most of them provide lines on which you write the important information. When filling out these cards, make sure that you have all the correct information and that the printing or handwriting is legible. It is often a good idea to get an extra package in case you make any mistakes and need to redo some of the cards. Letting your child fill out the invitations is a good way to get him/her involved. Just make sure to check over what your child has written. If you have a young child, just have him/her sign the card and you fill in the rest.

E-Mail Invitations

In this very busy world filled with technological wonder, you may wish to send invitations via e-mail. This will only work if you have the e-mail addresses of the invitees. One of the advantages to sending invitations this way is that you can type one and then "carbon copy" it to everyone else on your e-mail list. Many on-line services will allow you to choose colors and do some simple editing of the document before you send it. Color makes your invitation more interesting for the recipient. Think about who will be getting the e-mail before you use this option. If the person receiving the invitation is not someone who regularly checks her/his e-mail, you may not hear back in a timely manner or the person might miss the party.

Invitations (cont.)

There are many unique types of invitations you can send. These take a little bit more time but are usually appreciated by those invited. Some ideas follow.

Balloon Invitations

You can choose very large, deflated balloons. Stretch the balloon so it will be a bit easier for the recipient to blow up. Use a fine-point permanent marker to write the pertinent information on the balloons. Include a note with directions for blowing up the balloon to find out about the party. It is also a good idea to include a note with your name and phone number so the recipient can give you a call if the balloon doesn't inflate.

Puzzle Invitations

Children enjoy doing puzzles. To create a puzzle invitation, all you need is an invitation that you have created. Computer generated ones work well for this. Glue the invitation to light cardboard, cardstock, or construction paper. After it dries, cut it out into several pieces. (Note: Use larger pieces for younger children.) Then place the pieces in an envelope. As with the balloons, you might want to include a note with directions for putting the puzzle together and your name and phone number.

Postcard Invitations

A quick way to invite guests to a party is to use postcards. You may be able to find some that relate to the theme of your party. Postcards are an all-in-one way to write invitations without having to use envelopes.

Invitations *(cont.)*

When to Send Invitations

Once you have chosen a date for your party, you need to send invitations in a timely manner. Many people need at least two weeks in order to plan. Allow time for buying or creating invitations, addressing envelopes, and postal delivery.

Mailing Invitations

Addressing invitations correctly is important if you want your guests to receive them. This means that you need to have the correct name, address, city, state, and zip code on each envelope. You also need to include your return address. You may want to have your child help you address the envelopes. If this is the case, teach your child where to write the recipient's name and your return address. Then allow time for your child to practice before starting on the real envelopes.

Make sure the addresses are legible. If they aren't, they will not be delivered and you may not know until the party is long over why some guests did not attend. Using the correct amount of postage is also important. If you send oversized envelopes, you will need more postage than for standard-sized envelopes. If you send postcards, you will need less postage. Check with your local post office to be sure you use adequate postage. You might want to take

your child to the post office and let him/her choose one of the various commemorative stamps that are available. You may even be able to purchase stamps that relate to the theme of your party.

Party Roster

Guest/Parent(s)	Phone Number	Can Attend	Cannot Attend	Thank-you Note

Four-Fold Invitations

Given for _____

Given by _____

Date _____

Time _____

Address _____

_____

Phone _____

Please reply by _____

You're Invited

To a Party

16

Tri-Fold Invitations

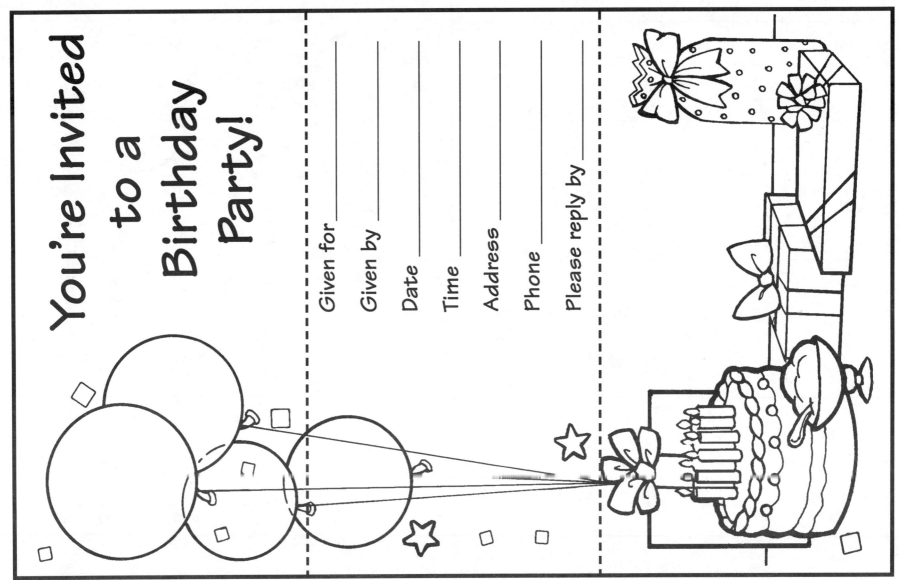

You're Invited to a Birthday Party!

Given for _____

Given by _____

Date _____

Time _____

Address _____

Phone _____

Please reply by _____

Party Helpers

You might want to have another adult, such as your spouse or a friend, help at the party. This way tasks can be divided up before the party begins. Another adult can also help supervise the children. This can come in handy if there is a sudden emergency situation. It also means that the children never need to be left unsupervised. Even if you know every child in attendance and each is usually a wonderfully behaved youngster, there's always the chance that someone will cause mischief, especially when in a group.

You might press into service other grown-up family members. A parent of a child who is attending the party is another option. Often parents would prefer to stay with their little ones, and depending on the age, they should. However, as children get older, parents often drop them off and leave. When inviting a child whose parent you think might like to help, ask the parent if he/she will be available. This can be done with a phone call or a note tucked into the invitation. You might want to give your helper a thank-you gift when you give out party favors to the children. Be sure to send a thank-you note after the party.

If someone you know is not able to help at the party, teachers from preschools or child-care centers are sometimes willing to work at children's parties for a fee.

Party Helpers *(cont.)*

While another adult is definitely important, you might also think about having a few younger helpers. If your child has older siblings, your help might just be built in. If not, think about recruiting some teenagers you know or babysitters you have used in the past.

These extra hands become invaluable when it comes to playing games, cutting cake, or opening gifts. These helpers often enjoy the party as much as the younger children! This will happen if you set a few guidelines. Assign them specific tasks, such as running a game or picking up the wrapping paper. If you hire them for the hours of the party, you might want to pay them as you would a babysitter. Determine what the fee will be before the day of the party when things might get rather hectic.

Presents

Thinking About Gifts

Children will bring gifts to birthday parties whether you want them to or not. It is part of the fun when children open gifts. It is also very important that you take care in preparing for this.

One of the most asked questions when you receive RSVPs from parents of those who can attend the party will be about the type of gift your child would like. Before this question is even asked, you should think about a response. You may want to check this out with your child. Ask: *Do you want action toys or board games? Is there a video you'd like to have?* You might just want to listen closely to your child and see if he/she mentions something that would make an appropriate gift. It might be a special stuffed animal or a cool pair of sunglasses. You may wish to share this information with parents who ask. However, check out the cost of anything before you mention it. It might be that your child is asking for something expensive and that could put you in an embarrassing situation.

You might also have some ideas of things you would like your child to receive. Books are always appropriate gifts. Children might not always suggest them, but they can appeal to every age group. They can also be inexpensive. Gifts related to your child's favorite storybook, cartoon, or movie characters make good gift ideas. While clothing doesn't appear at the top of a child's wish list, a T-shirt or sweatshirt with a favorite character on it makes an enjoyable gift.

Does your child have a favorite sport? Suggestions along these lines will make both the giver and recipient happy. Anything from a poster to tickets to a game can be an excellent choice for a gift.

Presents *(cont.)*

Receiving Gifts

Children may arrive at the party with gifts in hand. You need to have several things worked out before the first ring of the doorbell. Have a preselected spot to store the gifts until they are opened. This might be a special table, box, or basket that you have decorated.

If your child greets guests at the door, he/she needs to say thank you immediately. Then you or your child, depending on her/his age, can take the gift and put it in the designated spot, or one of you can show the guest where to place the gift. When your party is inside, this is generally easy to arrange since even a corner in a room will suffice.

If you are having your party some place other than a home, you will need to give this situation a little more thought.

- Keep the gifts in a specific location so they don't get lost.

- Be sure your child's gifts are not close to any other child's gifts if there is more than one party at the location you have chosen.

- If you are outside, at a park for instance, secure the gifts so they are not blown away by the wind.

- Never leave the gifts unattended.

- Make sure you have an easy way to transport the gifts. A box or basket works well for this.

When to Open Gifts

Opening gifts is often a highlight of a party. Children enjoy seeing what friends have chosen for the birthday child. Before the party begins, you should decide when your child will open the gifts. This can be based on many factors.

- Is your child one who won't be able to focus on having a good time until the gifts are opened? If so, you will need to open them early on.

- Do you want to clean up at the end of the party? Then you will need to open the gifts at the end of the party.

- Depending on where the party is held, you might even opt not to open gifts until after the party. In this case, pack them up and put them out of sight. Explain to your guests why you won't be opening gifts during the party.

Where to Open Gifts

Where to open gifts depends on where you feel comfortable with the mess created by wrapping paper and ribbons. It is nice to have a spot where all the children can view the gifts as they are opened. You might want to sit the birthday child in a chair and the other children on the floor. However, be prepared for the children to inch their way up to the child of honor. If you are outside, you might want to spread a large blanket on the ground so that everyone can sit on it.

Presents *(cont.)*

How to Open Gifts

Children love diving into a stack of colorfully wrapped gifts. They will take one and just start tearing it apart. Therefore, before the party begins, talk with your child about how to open the gifts. First, your child needs to know that gifts can be breakable so care should be taken when opening them. Next, explain that giving gifts is a very generous act and that no gift should ever be dismissed if it isn't exactly what your child wanted. Even if it's something that your child cannot stand, teach him/her to show good manners and say thank you in a polite way. More than any other moment during the party experience, here it is truly "the thought that counts."

Talk about opening cards first. Depending on your child's age, you or your party helper (page 18) may need to read the cards aloud. Always make sure that the giver's name is read aloud.

Have a pair of scissors on hand to cut ribbons that are uncooperative. A huge trash bag will be useful when it is time to clean up.

An easy solution to opening gifts and giving the giver some attention is to have that child bring his/her gift to the party child. Then the gift giver sits with the recipient as the gift is opened. A small sofa or piano bench works well. This is definitely a photo opportunity. Once the gift has been opened, the two children are photographed with the present. Enclosing this picture in the thank-you note gives it a special touch.

Presents (cont.)

Passing Gifts Around

Should you pass gifts around for children to take a closer look? You will need to determine that based on the age of the children. Generally, children under five will want to play with the toys, and that can cause a problem. Older children may genuinely want to look closer and know that they are not supposed to use the gifts. Here again, a party helper (page 18) can show the children the gift if having many hands touch it might cause a problem.

Recording Gifts

As gifts are being opened, the gift and the giver's name should be recorded as shown in the example below. This way when the time comes to send thank-you notes, it won't be difficult to remember who brought which gift. Once this information is recorded it can be attached to the Party Roster found on page 15.

Gift	Giver's Name
Cartoon Video	Alison
Puzzle	Nathan
Tickets to the Petting Zoo	Leticia
Coloring Kit	Tommy

Schedules

To make the day of the party run smoothly, create a party schedule. This can be as simple as writing a list of things you want to do, or you may want to make it more detailed by including the activities, when you want them to occur, and the name of the person responsible for each. Here are samples of each type of schedule. For your convenience, a Party Schedule form has been provided on page 26. Simply reproduce the form and plan your schedule. Write down as much detail as you like.

SAMPLE 1 — Simple List

Guests arrive. Have the childern decorate their own party bags.

Play games. (Clothespins in the Bottle, Pin the Tail on the Donkey, Over-Under Relay)

Open gifts.

Eat cake and ice cream.

Pass out party bags.

Parents pick up children.

SAMPLE 2 — Detailed List

Time	Activity & Person Responsible
2:00 P.M.	Guests arrive. Children decorate their own party bags. Sue helps. Bob takes photos and cleans up.
2:20 P.M.	Play games. Sue runs Clothespins in the Bottle and Over-Under Relay. Bob runs Pin the Tail on the Donkey.
2:50 P.M.	Open gifts. Bob records the gifts. Sue takes photos and cleans up.
3:10 P.M.	Cake and ice cream. Bob brings in cake and lights candles. Sue takes photos.
3:30 P.M.	Sue and Bob give out party bags as parents pick up their children.

Party Schedule Planner

Use the planner below to schedule the events of your party. You may wish to record the times as you see them happening. Keep in mind that these times are only approximate. If the children are enjoying themselves and need more time, be flexible and allow them to continue.

Time	Activity & Person Responsible

Thank-You Notes

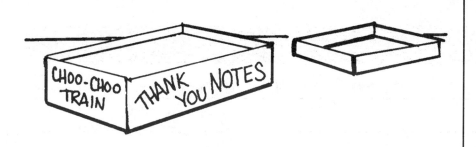

What to Say

The actual sending of the thank-you notes is most important, so the good news is they do not have to be lengthy. Make sure that the gift you are thanking them for is the gift they brought. This is where the list you made at the party becomes important. Mention that your child is enjoying the gift and that having their child as a guest helped make the day special. That's really about it, unless you can recall something unusual this child did at the party.

While it may be true that children don't expect a thank-you note from the birthday child, most parents consider it good manners to receive some recognition for taking the time to purchase a gift and transporting their child to and from your party. It is also a perfect opportunity for you to teach your child that thank-you notes are an important way of thanking others for their kindness and generosity. No matter how young your child is, she/he can take part in creating these notes. Your child may be able to write all of the notes from beginning to end or just sign ones you have written. If your child cannot write at all, consider having her/him help decorate the notes in some way.

Thank-You Notes *(cont.)*

Types of Thank-You Notes

Store-bought notes are fine. Make the task as easy on yourself and your child as possible. However, if you are up to it or your child is ready for it, homemade notes are a delight. If you took pictures of each child at the party and got doubles when they were developed, fold pieces of construction paper in half and glue the duplicates onto the fronts of the cards. Then write a short note inside each.

If you used stickers or stamps on your invitations, another idea is to use these again to decorate the thank-you notes. This will give your child a sense of theme.

It is fun for the recipient to have a tiny amount of glitter fall out when opening the thank-you note. However, don't overdo this because the parent won't appreciate having to clean up the mess.

Addressing Envelopes

If your child is old enough to write the thank-you notes, by all means, ask her/him to address the envelopes as well. This task can be a big chore, so the best way to handle this is to have your child do two or three a day.

However, unless your child has excellent handwriting, it is a good idea to address the envelopes yourself. After all, it doesn't do any good to write the thank-you notes if the postal workers can't read the addresses to deliver them.

Whether or not your child addresses the envelopes, invite her/him to help you place the postage stamps on them.

Sample Thank-You Notes

Here are examples of thank you notes. One is handwritten by a child, one is written by the parent and signed by the child, and one is a form to follow from a computer.

Dear Jo,
   Thank you for coming to my party. I really love the tee-shirt you gave me. I hope you had as much fun as me.
         your friend,
            Helen

Dear Eric,
   Thank you for the great truck. I will enjoy playing with it. Thanks for coming to my party. It was fun wasn't it?
      Your friend
         Jim

Where to Have a Party

Where should you have your child's birthday party? The possibilities are endless. There are only a few limitations. Ask the questions that follow to help you choose the best place to have your party.

- How many people will I invite?
- When will we have the party?
- What is the weather usually like during this time of year?
- Will I have to share the location with others?
- Is it near enough for those attending?
- Is it costly?
- Is it a place my child will enjoy?
- Is it safe?
- Will I need extra supervision?
- Does there need to be a large area so children can run around?

Once you have considered the above factors, there are a variety of places to have a party. Some possible party locations are shown on this page.

Possible Party Locations

- inside a home
- backyard
- pizza parlor
- restaurant
- museum
- circus
- gym
- farm
- park
- zoo
- bowling alley

- amusement park
- skating rink
- science center
- jewelry-making stores
- ceramic-painting stores
- college student union
- theater (movie or play)
- fun/discovery zone
- lake or ocean beach
- children's play center

    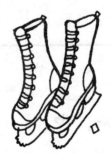 

Where to Have a Party (cont.)

Look at the list on page 30 for some places you might not have even considered as possible locations for your party. Call several weeks in advance to make reservations. Many places have party packages. If you are busy and do not have lots of time for planning, this might be the best option for you. Check out the location thoroughly to make sure that everything you want will be available. A few of the questions you might ask are listed below.

- What kinds of things will the personnel at the facility provide?
- What kinds of things will you need to bring with you?
- Is there a clean-up fee?
- Will there be games or some other kind of entertainment to keep the children occupied?
- Will one or more party leaders be provided by the facility?

Parks can be a great place for a party. Before making the decision to go to a park, call to find out what the rules and regulations are. The city, county, state, or federal government have parks that they maintain. Others are privately owned and operated. Each type of park probably has specific requirements as to what you may and may not do. Some parks require that you put down a deposit to reserve an area or equipment, such as a table and chairs, for your party. You want to avoid the disappointment of arriving at the park on party day only to find out that the picnic area you wanted is not available because you neglected to reserve it.

Where to Have a Party *(cont.)*

When deciding on a location, also keep in mind how children will get there. It is easiest if the location is relatively close and accessible so that parents can both drop off and pick up their child. If you have to transport children, you must make sure you have a seat belt for each child. Check the car seat laws. Think twice before driving children anywhere. Not only will you have the party to be responsible for, but you will also have the added anxiety of getting the children safely to and from the party site. This usually is not an ideal situation.

Remember that any location you choose for your party will have its limitations. If you have a child who wants to climb on things, run around, and roll on the ground, a party at a movie theater is not for you. However, a park may be an ideal place. Always keep safety in mind. You may need more chaperons if you go to a pizza parlor or the park than if you hold the party in your own backyard. Beach, lake, or pool parties require more supervision than other types of parties.

A special note for parents who want to "do it all": Your child may want the party at a particular spot. However, if making the arrangements to have the party at that location becomes too difficult or expensive, no one is going to have a good time. Only you can decide if the location is the best place for your child's party. If you find that the site your child has picked will not work out, explain that it would be best to have the party at home or another place of your choosing. Your youngster will be disappointed for a bit, but a successful party will make it all right in the end.

Decorations

Decorations set the mood for a party. The more festive the room, the more likely children arriving will be in the proper frame of mind to enjoy the party. Decorations can take all shapes and forms and can be made out of all types of materials. Before you consider decorations, you need to think about several things.

- Are you holding the party inside or outside?
- Will the weather be a factor?
- Can you hang decorations on the wall?
- Would you rather invest money in other aspects of the party?
- Do you want your party decorations to convey a theme?
- Is there a color scheme you want to follow?
- Do you want to coordinate all the party items, such as decorations, hats, table settings, etc., to go along with a particular theme or color scheme?
- How high do you want the decorations to be placed?
- What areas of the party location do you want to decorate?
- If the party is some place other than a home, what are the decorating policies?

Once you have had a chance to mull over some of these considerations, you can decide how and what to decorate. Some simple ideas for different types of decorations are provided on pages 34–38. Many of these can be made by

your child several days prior to the party. Having your child involved with creating the decorations will make preparing for the party more fun for both of you.

Homemade Room Decorations

Homemade decorations are a wonderful way to get your family involved with creating the party atmosphere. You will need to plan ahead so you have time to design and create the decorations, but these activities are a great way for your family to have fun together. Try making some of the decorations described on pages 34–40.

Paper Chains

Materials: construction paper, colored paper or brightly colored pages from magazines; scissors; cellophane tape, glue, or a stapler; masking tape

To Do: Cut lots of strips of paper about 3 inches (8 cm) long and ½ inch (1.3 cm) wide. These do not need to be exact. Take one strip and glue, tape, or staple the ends together to form a circle. Now take the next strip and place one end of it through the completed circle. Make another circle by fastening the ends of the new strip together. Continue until you have the chain as long as you want it.

Paper chains can be strung on the wall or across the ceiling. Secure the chains with masking tape. You may need to place a small piece of tape on links every few feet so the chain doesn't sag. If you are holding your party outside, hang the chains on a fence or tree branches.

Extras:

1. Choose two or three colors and create a pattern for your chains.

2. Use your chains to spell out the birthday child's name. Attach the paper chain letters to the wall.

Homemade Room Decorations (cont.)

Star Chains

Materials: star pattern or star-shaped cookie cutter; construction paper, wallpaper, or heavy wrapping paper; curling ribbon; scissors; hole punch or stapler; colorful or glittery markers (optional)

To Do: Use the patterns on this page or trace around a star-shaped cookie cutter to create paper stars. Cut out the stars. With a hole punch, make a hole near one point of each star and string curling ribbon through each hole. You can tie a loose knot in the ribbon after each star to keep them separated or just let them hang together. If you don't want to punch holes, simply staple the ribbon to each star. Hang the star chains with masking tape.

Extras:

1. Write the birthday child's name in the center of a star using colorful or glittery markers.

2. Let your birthday child draw pictures on the stars.

3. Write each guest's name on a star and let the children take the stars home as party favors.

Homemade Room Decorations *(cont.)*

Glittery Signs

Materials: paper to cover the table, poster board, pencil or marker, white glue in a squeeze bottle, glitter, tacks or pushpins, paintbrush (optional)

To Do: Decide with your child what the signs should say. "Happy Birthday" and "Welcome" are the obvious choices, but you may want to say things like "Joanna is 5 today! or "Let's celebrate Helena's 6th birthday!

Cover the work area with paper for easy clean up. Use the pencil or marker to write the words on the poster board. Try to keep the words all on one line or just put glue on one line at a time. Then, depending on your child's ability and your patience, let her/him use the glue to trace over the letters. A narrow paintbrush dipped into white glue works well for this. Once the glue is in place, have your child sprinkle glitter over it. Gently shake off the excess glitter. Continue until all the letters have glitter on them. Make sure the glue dries entirely before hanging up the signs. The signs can be tacked up or simply propped up against plastic soda bottles.

Extras: Use the marker to make bold outline letters. Instead of putting glue on the outline of each letter, use it to cover the inside. It may be easier to apply the glue with a wide paintbrush. Then have your child put the glitter on as described above.

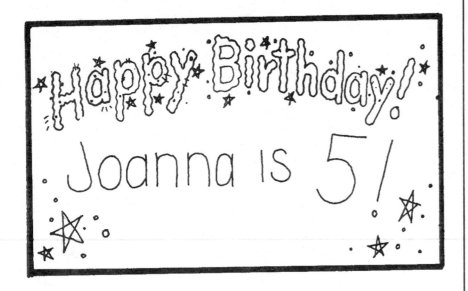

Berry Basket "Stars"

Materials: paper to cover the table; plastic berry baskets; scissors; white glue; paintbrushes; glitter; string, ribbon, or wire; masking tape

To Do: Start collecting berry baskets as soon as you can. Sometimes produce departments will give you extras. Then simply cut various shapes out of the baskets. Place them on a table that you have covered with paper. Use a paintbrush to lightly coat the different shapes with glue. Sprinkle glitter onto the wet glue. Shake off any excess glitter. Allow the glue to dry. Turn the shapes over. Lightly coat the other side of each shape with glue. Sprinkle the glitter onto the wet glue. Shake off any excess glitter. Let the glue dry. Then thread a piece of string, ribbon, or wire through each shape. Use masking tape to hang the shapes from the ceiling.

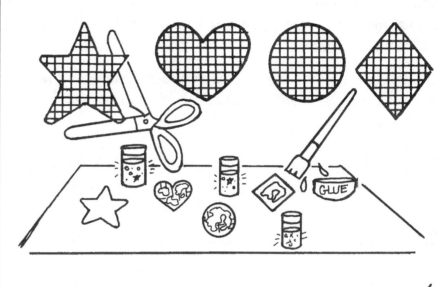

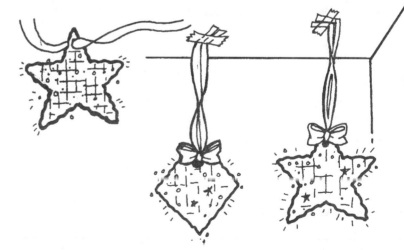

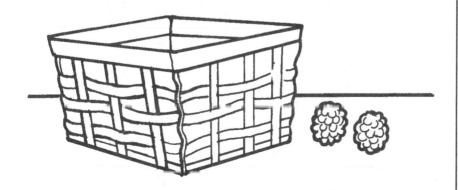

Homemade Room Decorations *(cont.)*

Paper Flowers

Materials: tissues, pipe cleaners, scissors, tape, plastic vase or container

To Do: For each flower, you will need two tissues and at least one pipe cleaner. Accordion-fold each tissue. Pinch each tissue in the middle and join the two together by placing the centers side-by-side. Twist the pipe cleaner around the two centers. Then spread out the folds on each end to create the flower. If necessary, use a bit of tape to connect the four pieces of the flower. You can extend the pipe cleaner stem by twisting additional pipe cleaners onto the one that holds the tissues together. Make several flowers using the above directions. Then place your flowers in a plastic vase for a floral decoration without the water.

Extras:

1. Use tissue paper rather than tissues to create the flowers. You will need to cut the tissue paper before using it. This will create bright and colorful decorations.

2. Use special scissors to create scalloped edges for the flowers. (See Snowflakes on page 39.)

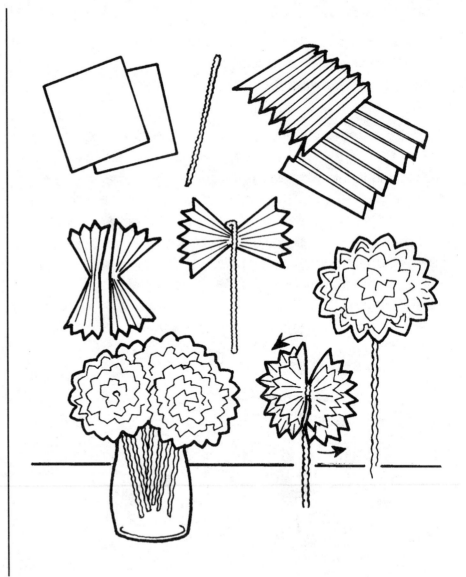

38

Homemade Room Decorations *(cont.)*

Snowflakes

Materials: square sheets of colorful paper (Origami paper works especially well.), scissors, crayons or markers, thin string or thin wire, masking tape

To Do: Fold the paper squares in half once and then in half again, creating a smaller square. Fold it in half a third time and then once more. If you were to open the paper, you would have 16 squares — but do not open the folds. Using scissors, cut small snips out of each corner. Now open the paper and you will have a colorful snowflake. Thread a piece of string or wire through one of the holes in the snowflake. Tie or twist the ends together. Secure the string or wire to the ceiling with masking tape so that the snowflake hangs down. You may wish to make several snowflakes to hang on a door jamb. Cutting the strings or wires different lengths will add to the effect.

Extras:

1. Let your child glue glitter or sequins onto the snowflakes for a glitzy effect.

2. Cut the snowflakes out of aluminum foil instead of paper.

3. Hang glitter or foil snowflakes with colorful ones for a special look.

4. There are many types of special scissors on the market. These will cut out edges that have various shapes such as scallops or squiggles. Use one or more different types of scissors to cut the designs for your snowflakes.

Piñata

Breaking a piñata is a traditional birthday activity in Mexico. Today it is used for many types of parties. You can make you own piñata. However, be sure that you do this several days before the party since it takes a long time to dry. Cover your work area with paper. You will need a very large balloon, some flour and water mixed up in a shallow pan for the paste, and lots of newspaper strips. Inflate the balloon. Then dip the newspaper strips into the paste and cover the balloon with them. After the strips have dried, use paint and paintbrushes or tissue paper and glue to decorate the piñata.

You can also purchase a ready-made piñata in many party or grocery stores. These come in a variety of shapes and sizes. You may be able to find a piñata that is tied to your party theme. Tell your child that part of the fun of having a piñata is breaking it apart. That way she/he will not be unhappy when the piñata is finally broken.

A piñata usually has a cavity with a hole on the top so you can fill it with candy and other small items. If you make your own piñata, you will need to cut the hole yourself. After you have filled the piñata with treats, suspend it from a tree or other suitable area. Then have the children take turns hitting it. A broomstick or plastic baseball bat works well for this. **Warning:** Wooden or aluminum baseball bats are too dangerous and should never be used to hit a piñata.

Traditionally, the child hits the piñata while blindfolded. However, if you do not have a large enough area or a sufficient number of grown-up helpers, do not use a blindfold. Most small children will not want to be blindfolded anyway. Let each child take three hits and then start over if the piñata hasn't opened yet. Once the piñata opens, the children will scramble for goodies. One way to be sure everyone gets a treat is to create bags of candy that are labeled with the children's names.

Store-Bought Room Decorations

Buying decorations for a party can be a great treat as well as a challenge! With so many choices, what does one choose? You are only limited by your imagination and your budget.

Balloons

What is it about a thin, bubble-shaped, incredibly light blob of plastic that floats in the air that makes so many people think of parties? It probably doesn't matter why, but many people wouldn't dream of having a party without balloons. Balloons and parties seem made for each other.

Warning: Be aware of the potential hazards balloons can cause. Never allow children to put balloons near their faces. If a balloon accidentally pops when it's near the child's mouth, the youngster could choke on it. If a balloon pops near the child's eye, it could cause an injury. In addition, the noise of popping balloons often scares young children. However, if you use caution, balloons can be a decorative asset to your party.

Store-Bought Room Decorations *(cont.)*

You can choose many types of balloons. They come in different sizes, shapes, and colors. Many party shops carry the type that say "Happy Birthday." Sometimes you can purchase balloons with information such as the birth year, child's age, or even personalized with the child's first name. Be sure to buy plenty of balloons since some will fail to inflate and others will pop while being inflated.

If you should choose to inflate the balloons by blowing them up yourself, be prepared for it to take quite a while (about a half-hour for 20 balloons). Remember, this process will take even longer if your child helps because you're sure to stop to bat the balloons around for a while.

With these balloons it helps if you stretch them out a few times before blowing them up. After blowing up each balloon, tie a knot in the end. Large grocery bags or plastic garbage bags make a good storage spot for the inflated balloons before you hang them up. This is also an easy way to transport them if you are going to be hanging them in different areas. When you are ready to hang up the balloons, attach them to the walls or ceiling using loops of double-stick tape or masking tape.

You may prefer to use balloons that are filled with helium. Party-supply stores, florists, and grocery stores often sell balloons that are already inflated. Check with these businesses regarding their prices, what type of balloons they have available, and their pick-up policy. Make sure the balloons are tied to pieces of string or ribbon and are weighted down before bringing them home.

Warning: Mylar balloons can cause major damage to overhead power lines. Do not leave the store until your balloons are secure.

Store-Bought Room Decorations *(cont.)*

If you wish to use helium to inflate your balloons, you will need to rent a helium tank. These tanks are usually available at party supply stores. You will need to check with the stores about their rental policies several weeks before the party. They may not have a tank available for the date you need it if you wait too long. Before you leave the store, make sure you really understand how to safely operate the tank.

Warning: Do not let children inflate the balloons using a helium tank. This work is for an adult.

Once you have your balloons inflated with helium, you can do several things. You can create balloon bouquets and have them float against the ceiling. The balloons can be tied individually around the children's chairs and each child can take one home. A few can be tied to the mailbox or a tree in front of the house to help guests identify where the party is being held. If you have a railing or banister, the balloons can be tied onto it. Outside they can be tied onto trees, bushes, or fences.

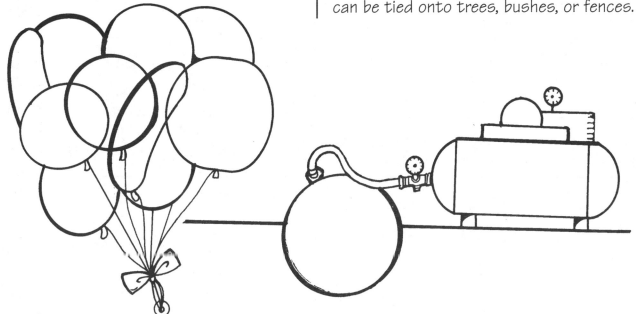

Crepe Paper

Crepe paper is wonderfully versatile when it comes to decorating. However, there are a few things you should remember. One is that you do not want to get it wet, or the color will run. So, while it can be used as a table decoration, you might want to keep it away from any beverages and water. Another thing to keep in mind is that crepe paper will droop after awhile, especially if it is heavy because you've used a lot of it. Therefore, you might not want to hang it too early. If it is used to decorate a wall, you may want to use some extra tape to keep it hanging the way you want it.

Use crepe paper to help decorate banisters, doorjambs, window frames, chandeliers, ceilings, walls, and the birthday child's chair. It is also pretty when draped over branches of trees. Several colors can be twisted together and strung across the ceiling. It can be looped and hung on a wall. The ends can be cut to form a "W" shape, and streamers can be placed in the middle of a table to add some color.

Crepe paper can be used to create a special entrance into the room where the party is held. Place a wide piece of masking tape across the top of the doorjambs, making sure that about a half an inch (1.25 cm) is hanging below the jambs. Then take crepe paper and cut or tear strips that will hang about a foot from the floor. Place one end of each strip onto the tape. Now take another length of masking tape and place it behind the back side of the crepe paper to secure the strips.

Use crepe paper liberally when decorating. A few rolls can go a long way. It easily complements other types of decorations.

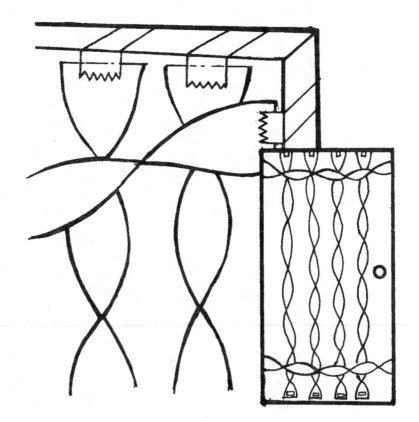

Store-Bought Room Decorations *(cont.)*

Signs and Banners

Signs that say "Happy 5th Birthday" or letters strung together with paper fasteners that say "Happy Birthday, Mike" often make a nice addition to the room decorations.

There are many types of these. A letter banner simply spells out words, while a flag banner has lots of pennants attached to each other and may show a word or symbol repeated over and over again. Some small signs are often attached to sticks and can be placed outside as a marker to designate the location of the party.

Banners or signs bought at party stores may be made of cardboard or lightweight plastic. Choose one based on what it says, how it looks, and how you can use it. One of the advantages of these signs is that they can usually be stored and used for another party.

Homemade Table Decorations

An inviting table makes it easier for children to use their very best manners. Even if you do not have enough room to seat all the guests at a table, it is still important for there to be a special place from which to serve the cake. Suggestions for table decorations are provided on pages 46–51.

Place Cards

Materials: construction paper, scissors, markers, stickers

To Do: Cut out construction paper rectangles and fold them in half. You can use almost any size of paper you wish. Use markers to write a party guest's name on each place card. Then decorate the cards with stickers. Put the cards on the table to designate each child's place.

Homemade Table Decorations *(cont.)*

Child-Decorated Tables

These are the best table decorations. They are a wonderful way for children to begin a party as participants in decorating the table. To see how this is done, look at page 60 for ideas.

Table Cutouts

Materials: various types of paper, paper tablecloth, templates or cookie cutters, glue, tape, stapler

To Do: With your child, create cutouts that can be taped onto the table or glued or stapled onto a paper tablecloth. Use any paper and shapes you like. You can create templates for the shapes, or you can trace around cookie cutters. In addition, you may want to cut out pictures from leftover party invitations or extra paper plates and napkins. Once you have created the cutouts, affix them to the top and sides of the tablecloth or table.

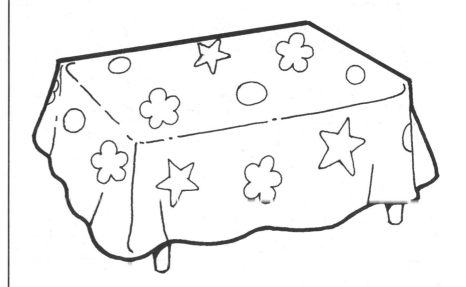

Homemade Table Decorations *(cont.)*

Paper Flowers

Materials: directions (page 38), tissues, pipe cleaners, scissors, tape, plastic vase or paper cups, and a nail

To Do: Create several paper flowers using the directions on page 38. Then place the flowers in vases in the center of the table. As an alternative to the plastic vases, you can use a nail to punch holes into the bottoms of paper cups. Then turn each cup upside down and poke a pipe cleaner stem through the hole.

Flowers

Materials: flowers, water, plastic vases or a clear plastic bowl

To Do: Fresh flowers can be a pretty addition to a table, especially if you are lucky enough to have a garden from which to pick some. However, if you have very young children, flowers may not make good decorations because they need to be placed in water, which can be spilled.

Also, keep in mind that if flowers are going to stay on the table while children eat, the arrangements need to be low so the youngsters can see over them. A simple arrangement for flowers is to just float a few of them in a clear plastic bowl.

Homemade Table Decorations *(cont.)*

Centerpieces

Materials: stuffed animals, toy cars, and/or special interest collections; shoebox, footed serving piece, or block of Styrofoam

To Do: A really personal centerpiece for a table may be one that represents your child's special interests. Does your child collect anything, such as small trucks or teddy bears? These can be made into an adorable centerpiece, one that is sure to please your child.

Invite your child to help you collect all the items that might work well as a centerpiece on the table. Place a platform, such as an upside down shoe box, footed serving piece, or a block of Styrofoam, on the table. Arrange the collected items on the platform. As an extra surprise for the birthday child, you might want to add a new item to the collection that he/she gets to keep after the party is over.

Store-Bought Table Decorations

Buying pretty decorations for a table is an enjoyable task. Just decide in advance what you need to decorate the table and set a budget. Crepe paper down the center of the table looks pretty, and doilies add a fancier touch. Special sparkling sequins that say "Happy Birthday" add a glittery touch to the table.

Crepe Paper

Twist together two colors of crepe paper and place them down along the center of the table. Make sure to tape them securely. You can also loop crepe paper onto the sides of the table, taping it in several places so it doesn't fall off.

Doilies

Doilies give a festive touch to almost any table. You can often purchase them (especially around the holiday time) in various colors. There are various sizes of round ones, but sometimes you can find them in heart or square shapes. These are most often found in the cake decorating section of party or craft stores.

Centerpieces

Centerpieces enhance the party table. Many of these use tissue paper that is honeycombed. These are usually folded in half for storage and then unfolded and connected with some type of clip for display. They look pretty and add a nice touch when placed on the table. Smaller honeycomb pieces can be put at each individual's place.

Place Cards

Both plain and decorated place cards can be purchased. Place cards work better when children are older and can read their own names. Write a guest's name on each place card. Let your child help you arrange the cards on the table before anyone arrives for the party. Place cards are pretty, as well as practical. Their use often cuts down on the squabbling about who gets to sit where.

Johnny

Table Coverings

You can buy paper tablecloths that are plain or already decorated. Using placemats, cloth tablecloths, or nothing at all are also options. In addition, butcher paper makes a handy table covering. The advantage of using paper is that the cleanup is so simple. After the party you just throw it all out. You can also have children decorate the table when they first arrive at the party. See the directions on page 60.

Setting the Table

Setting a party table can be lots of fun. Choose any of the decorations described on pages 46–51. Determine what utensils children will need. Remember, the fewer the better! Make sure to provide large napkins and lots of them.

The table is a good place to put hats and blowers for your guests. Hats can be fun, especially if children make their own (pages 52–54). Many children dislike the elastic that comes with store-bought hats and will not wear them for this reason. An alternative to putting the elastic under their chins is to put it behind their ears.

Blowers can provide amusement for older children. However, the noises that they make may scare young children, so think twice before using these with little ones.

Besides decorating the table, you can add some extras such as straws or ribbons tied around the beverage glasses. A candy stick makes a dandy beverage stirrer and looks festive on the table.

If you decide to have the children sit around the table, make sure you have enough seating for all of them. Folding chairs, piano benches, lawn chairs, and picnic benches can supplement your existing supply of table chairs.

Make Your Own Hats

Follow the directions below or on page 53 or 54 to have children create their own hats. They will enjoy wearing these because they have created the hats themselves.

Newspaper Hats

Materials: full page of newspaper for each hat; stapler, tape, or glue; scissors; crayons; paint and paintbrushes; stickers, glitter, feathers, and/or other materials for decorating

To Do:

1. Fold a full page of newspaper in half on the fold already provided.

2. With the fold at the top, pull the two corners down to meet in the middle. They will form triangles, ending about two inches (5 cm) from the bottom.

3. Fold the bottom edge up on each side of the hat.

4. To make the hat sturdier and more fitted for a child's head, cut the ends of the bottom band off and turn the band up one more time, or use a double thickness of newspaper.

5. You may wish to tuck in the ends of the band and secure them with a stapler, tape, or glue.

6. Let the children decorate the hats, using crayons, paints, stickers, glitter, feathers, and/or any other materials you have available.

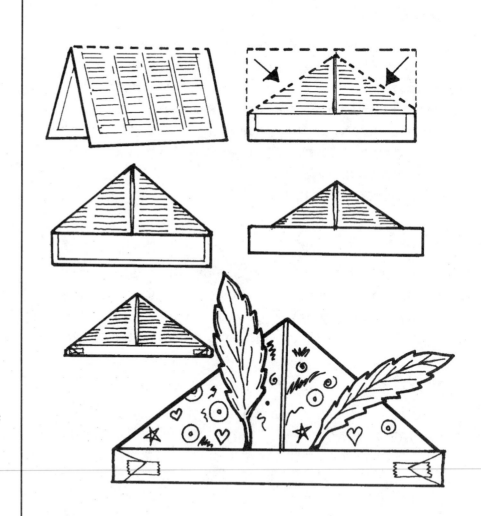

52

Make Your Own Hats (cont.)

For each child, trace the hat pattern shown below. Cut the hat out and punch the hole where indicated. Have the children color their hats and then fold and glue. Attach string ties so the children can wear them.

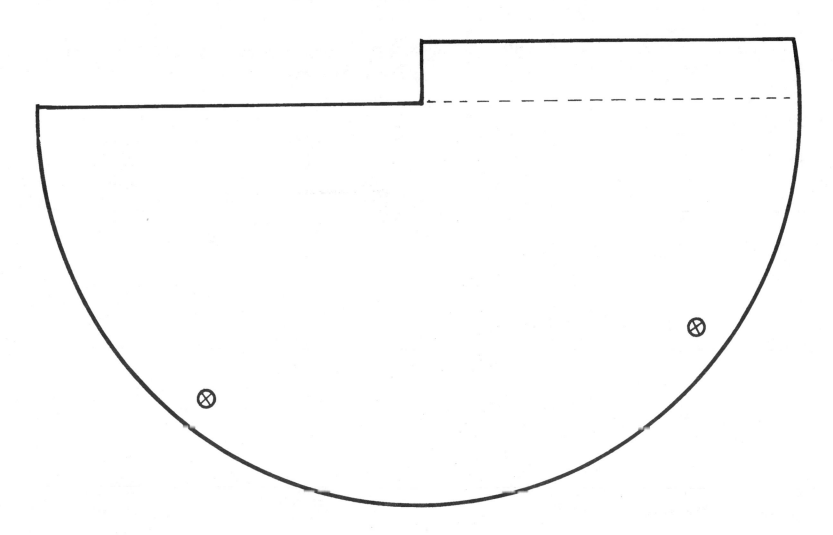

Party Headband Hats

These funny little headband hats are sure to please children as they wiggle their heads to and fro.

Materials: two 12–inch (30 cm) pipe cleaners, star patterns (at left), pencil, scraps of yellow construction paper, scissors, glue stick, glitter, plastic headband for each child

To Do: Starting about two inches (5 cm) from the center of each pipe cleaner, wind them around the pencil to make a short spring. Slip them off the pencil and put them aside. Cut four stars that are the same size from the yellow construction paper. (**Note:** You can choose shapes other than stars if you would like to make each hat a bit different.) Put glue on the stars and sprinkle glitter on the glue. Let the glue dry before shaking off any excess glitter. You may wish to write the children's names on the stars or use glue and glitter to write their names. Glue one end of each pipe cleaner between the undecorated sides of two stars. Allow the glue to dry. Then securely wrap the other end of each pipe cleaner around the headband.

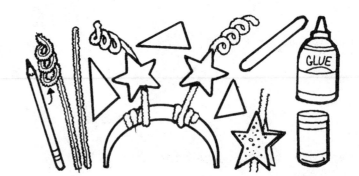

Computer-Generated Decorations

If you have a computer and some software that allows you to make banners and signs, you can create a lot of decorations for your party. There are many programs on the market that will allow you to do some of the things suggested below and on page 56. Take some time, long before the party begins, to become familiar with your computer program. It may save you time in the long run and help make your party a huge success.

Recommended Software

- Print Artist by Sierra for Win 95
  http://www.sierra.com/sierrahome/publishing/titles/paplat/
- Print Master by Mindscape for Win 95/98 and MAC
  http://www.mindscape.com/
- Print House by Corel for Win 95/98/NT and MAC
  http://www.corel.com/products/index.htm
- The Print Shop and The Print Shop Deluxe by Broderbund for Windows
  http://www.printshop.com/
- The Print Shop Publishing Suite by Broderbund for MAC
  http://www.livingbooks.com/store/product/24420.html
- American Greetings CreataCard by Broderbund for Win 95/98
  http://www.creatacard.com/

Banners

Banners strung across the room that say "Happy Birthday, James!" or "Welcome to Shameka's 6th Birthday!" are easy to make with the right software. You can select the font (type of print), colors, and, if you want, block or outline letters. Color printing can use a lot of ink in a relatively short amount of time. To avoid disappointment, have extra color ink cartridges for your printer on hand.

A way to get your child involved is to let her/him color the banner after you have printed it out with black outline letters. Invite your child to use crayons or markers to fill in the letters or outline them in a variety of colors.

Happy Birthday, Helena!

Welcome Sign

First-time visitors to your home often appreciate seeing a welcome sign on the front door. This lets parents who are bringing their children know immediately that they are at the right place. To create a sign like this you can use word-processing software. The sign can say something like "Welcome to Martin's party!"

Name Labels

Print out labels with the children's names to put on place cards. These can be printed in color and affixed to plain place cards, or they can be printed in black and put on colored or decorated place cards. Extra labels can be put on cups, so that they can be reused, or on party bags, for easy identification.

Clip Art Cutouts

Use clip art from your computer software to create cutouts. These can be used to decorate the table or the walls. You can often color these or have your child help you color them with markers or crayons. You can also scan in any of the clip art in this book. Then cut it out and color it.

As the Guests Arrive

You have called the party for 2 o'clock in the afternoon. The first guest arrives at 1:45, the next at 1:50 some come at 2, and a few latecomers get there at 2:30. What should you do while waiting for all the guests to arrive at the party? Should you just have the children sit and wait? With little children who are used to being busy and active, this is probably not a good idea. Giving them an activity to participate in after their arrival will keep everyone happier. On pages 57–63 you will find several ways to keep the children occupied until all of the expected guests arrive. While each child should be able to participate, those who come late may not have as much details to their projects as those who are arrive early.

Toys

Depending on the age of your guests, your child's own toys may be a great draw. Before you allow the guests to play with anything, clear it with the birthday child. Put away anything that either you or your child prefer others do not use. It's also a good idea to put the to-be-shared toys in boxes or baskets so they are accessible to all. (**Note:** Laundry baskets work well for this.) Using boxes or baskets makes for a quick cleanup when you are ready to start the more formal party activities.

Blocks and Legos

These standbys are terrific to have on hand. Little children love the thrill of creating cities, farms, and anything else they can imagine. Add a few action figures. You can keep them busy until everyone has arrived and you're ready to begin.

Party Bags

Chances are you will be giving children some type of party favors or small gifts before they leave. This is a nice gesture for the host or hostess as a way to thank the guests for coming. Putting that gift into a party bag makes it easier than wrapping it. You can purchase party bags or you can have each child at the party create one. If you have children do this when they arrive, at some point you or your helper can quickly place the goodies into the bags, so they are ready to distribute at the end of the party.

Materials: lunch or bakery sacks (plain white or brown are best for this); markers; crayons; pencils; glue; decorating supplies such as stickers, glitter, sequins, feathers, and stamps and ink pads; containers for supplies; name labels (optional)

To Do: You may wish to cover a table or work area with an old oilcloth, newspaper, or butcher paper. This activity works well when the children have plenty of room. Sometimes it is best for them to work on the floor. Place all supplies in containers in the middle of the room where children can easily reach everything. Multiple containers will eliminate the need for waiting. Let the children decorate the bags in any way they wish using the supplies you have available for them. Be sure each child's name is on her/his bag. Each child can write her/his own name, you can write it for the child, or you can use a name label that you have previously prepared. An oblong laundry basket or large department store box makes a good storage spot for the bags. This makes them easy to transport to any place you might need to take them. The beauty of this activity is that even the latecomers can at least add their names and some stickers while those children who come early can be very creative and add more details.

As the Guests Arrive (cont.)

Placemats

Materials: paper or construction paper cut to fit your table, prepackaged white placemats, or lacy placemats; crayons or markers; glitter; glue

To Do: Individual placemats that children create themselves often make the table a place they want to be. Coloring their own placemats makes for an enjoyable and often colorful table decoration. Give each child a placemat to color. Let the children use markers or crayons to draw whatever they want. Adding a bit of glitter helps to make the table sparkle. The lacy placemats look really pretty when placed over a colored tablecloth or bed sheet that is used to cover the table.

Make sure that each placemat bears the child's name. Either you or the youngster should write his/her name on the placemat. As an alternative, you may wish to use leftover computer name labels (page 56). Placemats are a big help when you need to sit children at more than one table or on the floor. The placemats mark their spots, and the children know immediately where they should sit.

If you want to make these placemats something that children can take home, precut tagboard the same size as the placemats. As the children finish decorating their placemats, glue each placemat onto tagboard and place a sheet of clear Contact® paper or self-laminating paper over it. Make sure the edges of the Contact® paper or self-laminating film fold onto the underside of the tagboard.

As the Guests Arrive (cont.)

Papered Table

Materials: butcher paper or white shelf paper, masking tape, yardstick, pencils, crayons or markers

To Do: Use butcher paper or white shelf paper to cover the table. Make sure to securely tape the paper to the underside of the table. Use a yardstick to draw a large grid, and write each child's name in a square on the grid. This becomes that child's square to decorate.

If you prefer, you can just let the children decorate the table any way they choose. This usually results in a riot of colors, something children love looking at. Be prepared with some ideas when you are asked the inevitable question, "What should I draw?" Answers like stars, cakes, animals, or rainbows will usually result in wonderful pictures by children. You might also wish to have on hand cutout shapes that children can trace.

Cupcake Cake

Materials: cupcakes of various flavors (without frosting), icings (various flavors), spreaders, all kinds of sprinkles, small decorative candies, cake plate, marker, candles, aprons or smocks

To Do: Let the children decorate their own birthday cupcakes, with no one asking for "more icing" or "nothing with pink on it." However, this is a messy project, so be prepared with aprons or smocks. (**Note:** Large, clean, old shirts put on backwards make good cover ups.) Let each child choose a type of cupcake. Write the child's name or initials on the bottom of the cupcake paper. Then have the youngster frost the cupcake. You may need to help the child get started by placing a large glob of icing on the cupcake. The child may opt to spread the icing or make it into a mountain on top of the cupcake. Encourage the child to decorate the cupcake by adding sprinkles and/or candles. When the masterpiece is finished, give the child a candle to place in the middle of the cupcake.

Place the birthday child's cupcake in the center of the cake plate. (**Note:** You may wish to cover the plate with doilies and use a special birthday candle for that cupcake.) Then place all the other cupcakes around the birthday child's cupcake. You now have a wonderful birthday cupcake cake.

As the Guests Arrive (cont.)

Treasure Hunt

Materials: lots of yarn or ribbon; paper towel tubes or sticks (one per child); small "treasures," such as pens, combs, or pairs of character or seasonal socks (one per child); scissors

To Do: Determine the path you want the children to follow when searching for their treasures. With young children, you may want them to go only a few feet, while older children may be allowed to venture into many different rooms. (**Note:** To avoid confusion, it is helpful to use different colored yarn or ribbon for each child.) Tie one end of the yarn or ribbon around a paper towel tube or stick. Leave the tube or stick where the child is to start the treasure hunt.

Leave a trail of yarn or ribbon as you walk the path you have chosen. When you get to the end of your path, tie the treasure onto the other end of the yarn or ribbon and leave it there. You will need to follow this procedure for every guest. You may want to add a nametag to each paper towel tube or stick — still another use for the computer-generated name labels (page 56). Have the child wrap the ribbon around the tube while following the path.

Keep a pair of scissors handy. This way, if children get really mixed up all you need to do is snip the yarn or ribbon and help them roll it back onto their paper towel tube or stick. Expect confusion (and hilarity) as the children follow the treasure trail.

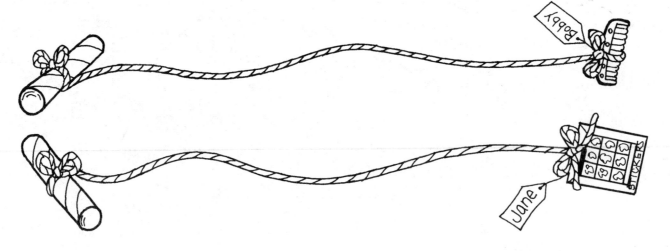

As the Guests Arrive *(cont.)*

Treasure Boxes

Materials: small white boxes (These can be obtained at most craft supply stores.); stickers; markers; crayons; glitter; glue; small "treasures" such as stickers, plastic necklaces, toy cars, or plastic dinosaurs

To Do: Give the children plain white boxes to decorate. Let each child decorate the box with materials you provide. Make sure the child's name is written somewhere on the box. When the boxes are finished, add a small "treasure" to each for the children to take home.

Party Food

There are probably as many types of foods to serve at parties as there are types of parties to have. The trick is to make the food for a child's party simple and kid-friendly. Cake and ice cream are traditional, but you do not always need to serve these. Check with your child. While a three year old may not be concerned about what is served, a seven year old certainly will be. Maybe the birthday child wants an ice cream cake or no cake at all. If your child has allergies to certain foods, it wouldn't be fair to serve all the guests something that she/he cannot eat. Be sure to make the food for the party revolve around your child's needs and favorites. You will need to do some planning before the day of the party.

To make the task easier, begin by asking yourself several questions.

- Will the children need anything to eat at all?

- Am I going to serve ice cream and cake?

- Will I be serving breakfast, lunch, or dinner?

- Do I need to consider healthy food choices for this party?

- Have I included my child's favorites?

- What will I serve to drink?

- How much time do I want to spend preparing food?

- Am I aware of any food allergies that I may need to take into consideration?

- How much money do I want to spend on the food?

These are just the first questions you will want to ask yourself. Once you have the answers, you can begin to plan. Read through pages 65–71 for ideas of types of foods to serve. Once you have decided, use the menu planner on page 72 as a worksheet and a grocery list.

64

Party Food (cont.)

Kid-Friendly Foods

What is a kid-friendly food? It is basically a food that a child will eat and enjoy. Often it is something that can be eaten with hands, rather than utensils. These foods are not anything new and exotic. (Remember, many children think that anything other than peanut butter is exotic!) They do not necessarily fit into the nutritious category, so if this is an important consideration, you may need to modify some of the items. For example, you could substitute a veggie burger for a hamburger. If you are planning to serve more than ice cream and cake, you might want to consider some of the following foods for your party.

Munchies and Nibblers: chips, pretzels, celery and/or carrot sticks, candy

Sides: cheese wedges or sticks; string cheese; bread sticks; peeled fruit slices, including peaches and oranges (Don't use anything that turns brown or squishy!)

Main Dishes: sandwiches (with or without crusts), including peanut butter and jelly, turkey, and roast beef; hamburgers and/or hot dogs on buns; pizza

Desserts/Sweets: animal crackers, cookies, root beer floats

Beverages: sodas, milk, juice, punch, lemonade, white grape juice, slushes

Serving a Meal

If you have decided to serve a meal, there are a lot of quick and easy ways to do this that will make it a memorable experience for the children and easy for you to prepare and clean up.

You can, of course, opt to have your meal prepared by a local fast-food restaurant. Often this is part of the package that you buy when you book a party at one of these establishments. This is the quickest and simplest way for you since there isn't any preparation or clean–up involved.

If you are having the party at home or elsewhere, you can often work out an arrangement for meals to be prepared and picked up so you can serve them at the party. It is a good idea to call a few days before the party to work out details such as how much it will cost an adult and how to pay for the food. Here's an area in which a party helper (page 18) who can pick up the meals for you would be of tremendous help.

Party Food (cont.)

If you choose to make your own meals for the party, here are some easy ways to serve them.

Platters

Make large platters of everything. You or your helper should walk around and serve them. This will work whether the children are at a table or on the ground, as long as they are sitting. As an alternative, you may wish to put the platters onto a buffet table and let children help themselves. To avoid problems, such as a peanut butter lover refusing to eat a sandwich because it touched a turkey sandwich, be sure to separate the different things. (**Note:** Older children can pass the platters themselves if you don't mind, but you'll need to help out the little ones.)

Lunch Sacks

Use lunch sacks or party bags to pack an individual lunch for each child. Wrap each item separately. If you are serving sandwiches, then make lunches with different sandwiches and ask children which one they would like. Keep your choices simple. Using the colored plastic wrap that is now readily available in most stores makes the lunches pretty to look at.

Plated Meals

When you eat in a restaurant, your food generally comes plated — that is, all together and portioned on the plate. Do this with the children, being careful to put the same number of items on each person's plate. The plates that are divided into sections can make this easy. These types of plates also help with that child who just won't eat anything if one type of food touches another.

Party Food (cont.)

Making the Food Attractive

Food for children is often eaten quickly or not at all, but it is still nice for them to see that it is attractively prepared. Often what makes a party special is to have food that is different from what is eaten on a daily basis. Below and on page 69, you will find some ideas for ways to make food fun to eat.

Sandwiches

- Cut off the crusts.

- Instead of cutting sandwiches in half, make them into triangles or squares.

- Use cookie cutter shapes to cut out the bread.

- Make a loaf sandwich. Place one piece of bread, then a filling, then another piece of bread, then another filling, then another piece of bread, and so on. These might need to be held together with toothpicks.

- Use party picks to hold sandwiches together. You can often get these to go with the theme of your party.

- Use mini bagels and colored cream cheese.

Main Dishes

- Serve individual pizzas.

- Make faces on the pizza with olives, cheese, pepperoni, or anything else that sounds appealing.

- Make English muffin pizzas.

Party Food (cont.)

Vegetables and Fruits

- Make carrot curls. Use a vegetable peeler to cut long strips of carrots. Curl the strips. Then use a toothpick to hold each curl. Place the curls in a bowl of ice water in the refrigerator for at least an hour. Take out the toothpicks and serve.

- Cut vegetables very thinly or into matchbox strips.

- Make fruit kabobs by placing a piece of banana and an orange slice onto a toothpick. Repeat the pattern three times per pick.

- Add food coloring to cream cheese. Then spread the colored cream cheese into celery sticks.

Beverages

- Make ice cubes before the party, placing a maraschino cherry in each one before freezing. Serve these in the beverages.

- Use a little food coloring in clear beverages, such as lemon-lime soda or lemonade.

Party Food (cont.)

Ice Cream and Cake

You can serve ice cream and cake as refreshments at any birthday party. The two go together so well! Since this is a special moment for your child, make sure the cake is special too. Begin by asking your child which type of cake is his/her favorite. However, if he/she answers carrot or something else that you think the guests might not like, you may want to have two cakes — the one you think should be served at the party and the one your child wants!

There are many ways to handle the cake, from buying one at the store with all the decorations to making one from scratch. There are also lots of options in between.

Bakery Cakes

Ordering a cake from a bakery can be as simple as a phone call if you know exactly what you want. This works well if you have used the bakery before and they do not need a deposit. Whether you order over the phone or in person, there are certain things the bakery will need to know. These include the type of cake, type of icing, size (determine this by how many people you need to serve), number of layers, colors, types of decoration, and the date you need to pick it up.

If you want an elaborate decoration, you are probably better off going to the bakery to order the cake. A picture or drawing of what you want can be very helpful. If you haven't decided on a decoration, most bakeries have pictures of designs from which you can choose. Whether you have something specific in mind or not a clue, plan to spend some time at the bakery explaining what you want.

Sometimes a bakery will make the cake layers or cupcakes without frosting them. Then you can frost and decorate the cake yourself or have the children frost and decorate the cupcakes (page 61). For either of these options, you will need some time for a special order.

Homemade Cakes

Baking a cake takes time. Perhaps you have an old family favorite that has appeared at every one of your family's parties. Maybe you have an idea for special decorations that you know your child will adore. If you opt to bake the cake, just make sure to give yourself plenty of time. It's not only the baking that takes time — it's the planning, the shopping, the cooling, the frosting, the decorating, and the clean up. Having your child help you make the cake can make this a rewarding experience, especially when you see those little eyes light up!

All sorts of cake mixes are available. Make sure to follow the directions on the box, including the one that tells you to let the cake cool before frosting it. It's not a bad idea to make this a two-day project so the layers are completely cool. Children can be very disappointed if the icing doesn't stick.

You can make icing from a favorite recipe or a mix, or you can buy the ready-made kind. Any of these can be used on any kind of cake. Just make sure you have enough icing to frost the type of cake you are making. If you buy containers of frosting, then it might be wise to buy two to make sure you have enough.

Once the frosting is on the cake, you can add decorations. Some things to add include frosting or sugar flowers, sprinkles, candies, and cookies. You can use inedible decorations, such as candles and plastic figures, if you make sure to remove them before the cake is cut.

Be aware that if you add something like frosting or sugar flowers to the cake, there is a large possibility that most or all of the children will want to have them. You might add enough so that this is a possibility. You can simply pick them off and put them on each child's cake plate or you can cut the cake so each piece includes one.

Menu Worksheet

Menu for _____'s Birthday Party on _____.

(Name)   (Date)

We will serve:

We already have on hand:

We need to buy:

We need to pick up these things **before the day of the party:**

We need to prepare these things **before the day of the party:**

We need to pick up these things **the day of the party:**

We need to prepare these things **the day of the party:**

Picture Taking

Stills

Purchase rolls of film that have 36 prints so you can take plenty of photographs. Party pictures become an important part of your family's history. This is one time to snap away, because your child will be happy and won't feel self-conscious. Take a few pictures of the activities and don't forget those special decorations you spent so much time creating. Get a picture of the cake. But most of all, move in close when you're taking photos of your child and the guests. If you have a zoom lens, use it. Your most treasured pictures will be of your child at this particular age, so you want to see her/him clearly. If your child is wearing a special costume or face makeup, take a few extra photos. This is truly a once-in-a-lifetime experience. If you're too busy supervising the party to take pictures, designate someone to be the photographer. It is helpful if this person has some experience with your camera. Ask the photographer to move in as close as possible.

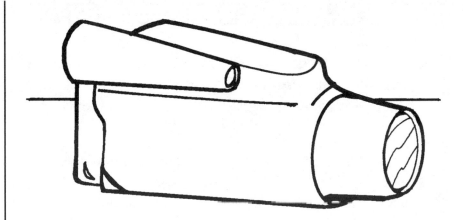

Video

If you like to have videos, by all means take some. These are a bit more problematic than stills. A few minutes of video usually go a long way. There is often a great deal of dead time on them, and rarely does anyone besides your immediate family ever want to see them. They can also create anxiety for the parent who is attempting to video as well as keeping the party moving. You might be tempted to call for "action" just when the party-goers feel like taking a break. Try to get a friend to relieve you from video duty. Tell the videographer what parts of the party are essential to record and give her/him free rein on the rest. You'll enjoy what is captured on the video and have a much better time at your child's party when you're not trying to be Steven Spielberg.

Unexpected Situations

Someone once said, "Always expect the unexpected." This is truly the case with little children. However, if you are prepared, you can often defuse certain situations and learn to cope with others. Remember, some things are the parents' doing, not the children's. For instance, do not become angry with children if their parents are two hours late to pick them up.

If parents aren't staying with their children, make sure that you know where and how to contact them. If they will not be at home, ask for a phone number where you can reach them in an emergency.

A child gets hurt or becomes ill

Call the child's parents immediately. Deal with the situation as best you can. If it is an extreme emergency, you may need to call 911.

A parent doesn't pick up a child

You cannot leave a child unattended. You will need to wait with the child until the parent shows up. To help avoid this type of situation, inform parents of a specific ending time for the party.

A child gets teased for not bringing a gift

Bringing a gift to a party is always implied, but it is not necessary. You may need to dissuade children if they say unkind things by reminding them that the purpose of the party is to have fun together and celebrate the birthday child, not to get gifts.

Unexpected Situations *(cont.)*

A child is allergic to the food or beverages you are serving

Hopefully, parents will tell you about this before they leave their child with you. However, you need to ask. When parents call to R.S.V.P. for the party, it is perfectly okay to ask them if their child has any food allergies or dietary restrictions. Also, many children will be able to tell you which things they can't eat.

Someone who said he/she wasn't coming shows up at the last minute

Always try to buy a few extra plates, blowers, and favors so that if this happens, it won't be a problem. Set an extra place at the table. If you do not have enough party favors and you bought one for your birthday child, he/she might be willing to give it up since he/she has received some gifts.

Other children pick on a particular child

You may need to step in and just ask the others to be kind to each other. Another option is to ask the child who is being picked on to be your special helper. For example, you could ask this child to help you serve the cake or hand out prizes. This will give the youngster some attention and get him/her away from the others.

Crafts make good birthday party activities. Each child gets to create something unique. The guests get to take something home with them as a reminder of the day's events.

Painting Clothing

While children won't have the time to sew their own clothing, painting clothing to take home is a fun project for a birthday party. Your best bet is to buy plain colored clothing that doesn't have any decoration on it. Caps, visors, T-shirts, and socks all make good items for painting. Use fabric paint so it will stick. Make sure you read the manufacturer's directions before the party so you will know what to do.

Materials: butcher paper, masking tape, items of clothing (one per child), pieces of cardboard or magazines for shirts, pencils, fabric paints, paintbrushes, squeeze bottles (optional), access to water for clean up

To Do: Cover the work surface with butcher paper. Tape it down. If the children are painting T-shirts, place a piece of cardboard or a magazine inside each so they do not paint through to the back. You can tape the excess part of each T-shirt onto the back of the cardboard or magazine so it doesn't get painted. If the children are painting socks, make sure the cuffs are rolled down so

the paint will show. Explain to the children that painting the bottom of the sock is not a very good idea. Let the children use pencils if they wish to sketch a design on the clothing they plan to paint. Then they can use the fabric paint and paintbrushes to paint over the design. However, using squeeze bottles may make the painting easier. Some paints come in these. It's a good idea to demonstrate how to paint so children don't mix the colors into a homogenized mess. Painting should be done early on in the party. This gives the projects a chance to dry so children can take them home when they leave.

Crafts (cont.)

Clay

Clay projects are fun no matter when you have them scheduled during the party. Clay can be shaped into many different items. A project that many children enjoy making with clay at birthday parties is a birthday cake. You may wish to use commercial modeling clay, play dough, or one of the recipes provided below for homemade play dough. If you are making your own clay, make it well before the guests arrive. For easy cleanup, let the children work on a butcher-paper covered tables or cutting boards covered with wax paper. Provide tools, such as craft sticks, rolling pins, cookie cutters, and plastic knives, that allow them to work with the clay.

Play Dough

Ingredients
2 cups (480 mL) flour
2 cups (480 mL) water
2 tablespoons (30mL) oil
1 cup (240 mL) salt
2 teaspoons (10mL) cream of tartar
food coloring (optional)

Directions

Mix all ingredients together in a saucepan. Cook and stir until mixture thickens and starts to stick to pan. Knead out the lumps. Cool completely. Store tightly covered. This makes enough for about 10 children.

No Fail Play Dough

Ingredients
1½ cups (360 mL) flour
¾ cups (180 mL) salt
1½ cups (360 mL) water
1½ tablespoons (22.5 mL) cooking oil
food coloring

Directions: Sift the dry ingredients together into a bowl. Mix the liquids in a pan, and add the food coloring. Pour the dry ingredients into the liquid mixture. Cook the batter over a low to moderate heat, stirring constantly until the thickened mixture begins to loosen from the sides of the pan. Remove the dough from the pan and knead it; allow the dough to cool. Store the dough in a plastic bag or airtight container; it does not need refrigeration.

Games

Getting to Know You Games

Sometimes children come to a party knowing each other. Other times they do not. You may wish to play some ice breakers with them so that they get to know each other a little bit better. Some suggestions are provided below and on pages 79–81.

My Name Is _____, and I Like

_____.

Have the children sit on the floor in a circle. First, provide a category. Food and animals are generally easy ones for children. Then have your child say, "My name is _____, and I like _____." Have your youngster fill in the blanks with his/her name and something that he/she likes from the category you have named. Go around the circle and have each child do this once. Then see if each child can name the other children and what they liked. To make this simpler, have the children give only their first names. To make it more difficult, have them say something in the category you pick that begins with the same letter as their first names.

Getting to Know Me

This game takes some simple preparation and is best for children who can read. If the children are nonreaders, then read the items to them and let them find another party-goer that fits each description and shake hands.

Materials: game boards (page 79; one per child), pencils (one per child)

To Do: Reproduce the game board for each child. Give each child a pencil. When you give the signal, have each child find someone who fits the description in each square on the game board. Once a child has found someone who fits a particular description, that person should sign his/her name in that square. Tell children that all the squares may not be filled in at the end of the game. They may also have a child sign more than one square, but it's more fun if they don't.

Has a pet	Likes dinosaurs	Has a name spelled with three letters	Read a book this week
Plays a sport that you also play	Is in the same grade as you	Has gone on a vacation	Watched a movie yesterday
Likes to eat chocolate ice cream	Goes to your school	Has a little brother or sister	Has a computer at home
Rides a school bus	Has lost a tooth	Likes to eat pizza	Is wearing something blue

Games *(cont.)*

Getting-to-Know-Me Game Board

Find someone who fits one of the descriptions in the boxes. Ask that child to sign his or her name in the right box. Try to get a different child's name in each box. Continue playing until you have names in as many boxes as possible.

Has a pet	Likes dinosaurs	Has a name spelled with three letters	Read a book this week
Plays a sport that you also play	Is in the same grade as you	Has gone on a vacation	Watched a movie yesterday
Likes to eat chocolate ice cream	Goes to your school	Has a little brother or sister	Has a computer at home
Rides a school bus	Has lost a tooth	Likes to eat pizza	Is wearing something blue

The verbal games described on pages 80 and 81 can be played without any materials. They are especially fun at the end of a party, as children wind down. The idea is to have fun, so if one seems too difficult, go to another.

I Spy

Find an object in the room. Then say, "I spy something that is _____ ." Fill in the blank with one characteristic of the object, such as its color or shape. Let the children take turns guessing what the object is. After each round of guesses, give a new clue.

Go Togethers

There are many things that we associate as "go togethers" or pairs. For instance, if you say "up" someone may say "down." Try this with your party guests. Here are several to get you started: cat and dog, soap and water, night and day, shoes and socks, bat and ball, horse and cart, girl and boy, bread and butter.

Opposites

Call out a word and see if the children can give you its opposite. Here are some to help you get started: sad and happy, hard and soft, dirty and clean, cold and hot, light and dark, short and tall, under and over.

I Start With _____.

Think of a category, and give the children a letter or let them choose one. Then ask the children to tell you the names of items that fit into that category and begin with the specified letter. Some categories include cars, television shows, athletes, food, toys, flowers, colors, and animals.

Games (cont.)

Brainstorming

With this simple game, children unlock their ability to think quickly. You'll be amazed how even young children can think up answers. Give the children a topic and ask them to name as many ways as they can for people to use something. For instance, ask the children to name as many ways as possible that people use numbers. You might give them a few examples, such as phone numbers, addresses, or writing checks. Give them a couple of minutes to think. Then watch them go to town! Other questions to ask include the following: What kinds of things can you do with a cup? What can you use a pencil for, besides writing? What kinds of things can you do with a straw, besides drink from it?

Rhyme Time

Give children words that you know they can rhyme. After you say a word, have them name rhyming words. For young children, use simple words, such as *cat, car,* and *big.* With older children make the words harder or use more syllables, such as *funny, bumpy,* or *silly.* Let children make up words if they want to.

Initials

This is a great game for the older set. Give the children a first and last initial of a famous person or someone in the party room. It's often fun to start with the birthday child. Then have the children guess whose initials these might be. They can ask questions that are answered with "yes" or "no."

Do I Belong?

This is a good listening game. Write a list of categories. Then choose one. For instance, if the category is cars, you could say *wheel, engine, doll, tires.* The children should call out that *doll* is the one that doesn't belong.

Traditional Games

These traditional games (pages 82–86) have been played and enjoyed by children for many years. They require little preparation. To speed these games along, a party helper (page 18) comes in very handy. It's often a good idea to let the birthday child go first, so spend some time before the party explaining the games to your child.

Pin the Tail on the Donkey

You can purchase a game commercially or create one of your own. The directions given below can easily be adapted for many themes (pages 92–160).

Materials: poster of a donkey without a tail; tape; tails, each with a guests name written on it; blindfold

To Do: Tape the poster to the wall at a height that a child's arm will touch when reaching straight out. Use the tape to make a line on the ground. Ask the children to wait behind the line. You may wish to have the birthday child stand first in line. Give each player a tail with her/his name on it. Place some tape on the back of the first player's tail. Then blindfold that child and gently turn her/him around in a circle. Tell this youngster to walk while holding the tail with an outstretched arm. Once the child touches a wall, she/he needs to leave the tail in that spot. The winner is the one who gets the tail closest to where it should be on the donkey.

Note: Many young children do not like to be blindfolded or turned around in a circle. If this is the case, don't insist that they get turned around or play the game. It is also important that you clear the area where the children are playing, and you keep those waiting for their turn behind the line. If you have a helper, have that person get the next child ready for her/his turn.

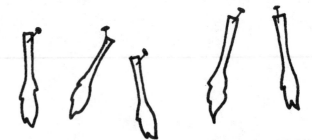

Traditional Games *(cont.)*

Drop the Clothespins in the Bottle

Materials: tape, wide-mouthed jar or bottle (A mayonnaise jar works well for this.), 5–10 clothespins, sturdy high-backed chair

To Do: Use the tape to draw a line and place the children behind it so they can each have a turn. The line can be to the side of the bottle so the guests can see what is happening. Have one child at a time kneel on the chair, facing the back. The bottle should be placed on the floor behind the chair. Hand the kneeling player one clothespin at a time, and have him/her try to drop each into the bottle. (**Note:** Pick the number of clothespins based on the age of the children.) All children should try to drop the same number of clothespins into the bottle. To speed things up, you can have two games going simultaneously. The child who drops the greatest number of clothespins into the bottle is the winner.

Three-Legged Race

Materials: scarves, old ties, or torn up sheets

To Do: In this race, two children race as one person with three legs. Have the children partner up and stand next to each other. Tie their inside legs together — not too tightly — with a scarf, old tie, or strip of sheet. Say "Go" to begin the race.

Shoe Scramble

Materials: all the children's shoes

To Do: Have the children take off their shoes and place them in a large pile. Mix up the pile. When you say "Go," the children should race to the pile, find their own shoes, and put them on. The winner is the child who puts on his/her own shoes first.

Over-Under Relay

Materials: one ball per team

To Do: Divide the children into a minimum of two teams consisting of at least five players each. If the groups aren't even, you or your party helper (page 18) may need to play. Have the children line up by teams. Hand a ball to the first child in each line. The first child passes the ball over her/his head to the next child. The second child passes the ball between her/his legs to the next child. The third child passes the ball over and so on. When the last child in line gets the ball, she/he runs to the front of the line and the whole process begins again. When each child has been to the front of the line, the team sits down. The first team to sit down is the winner.

Note: A ball is likely to fall out of someone's hands. Help the children get the ball back and start from where they left off.

Follow the Leader

Line up all of the children with the birthday child in front. Put on some marching music and have the birthday child begin by marching and then do something like jumping on one foot or waving. The other children need to do the same thing. When you determine that all the children have followed the leader, the leader moves to the back of the line. Then the next child becomes the leader.

Traditional Games (cont.)

Put the Cotton Balls in the Bowl

Materials: large bowl, one package separated cotton balls, spatula, blindfold, pencil and paper (optional)

To Do: The first participant kneels in front of the bowl and cotton balls. Place the blindfold over the player's eyes. Then put the spatula into one of his/her hands. Tell the child to place the other hand behind his/her back. Choose a certain number of times the child can attempt to pick up the cotton balls with the spatula and place them in the bowl. After each child's turn, count the number of cotton balls in the bowl. Then remove them. Keep track of the scores by writing them down or having each child remember his/her own. The winner is the child who gets the greatest number of cotton balls in the bowl.

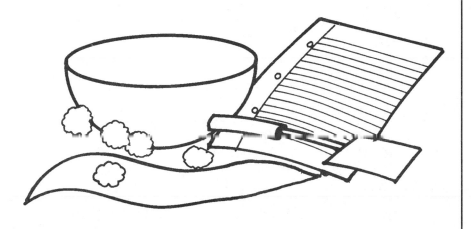

Duck, Duck, Goose

This is a game for young children. Have them sit in a circle. One child is "it" and walks around the outside of the circle gently tapping each child on the head. As the circling child does this, he/she says, "duck, duck, duck, duck, goose." The child can say "duck" as many times as he/she chooses. Whoever gets called "goose," jumps up and chases the other child around the circle. The "goose" tries to touch the other child on the arm or back before he/she sits in the goose's spot. If the child who is "it" gets back to the goose's spot without being touched, the "goose" is "it" and begins the process again. The play is over when everyone has had a turn to chase and be chased or the game begins to lag. This game can easily be adapted to other types of parties such as "Car, Car, Truck" for the Cars and Trucks Party (pages 97–100) or "Bear, Bear, Goldilocks" for the Fairy Tale Party (pages 123–133).

Traditional Games *(cont.)*

Musical Chairs

This game requires one less chair than the number of children playing. Place the chairs back-to-back. Play music that you can easily turn off. Then have all the children stand in front of the chairs. When you begin the music, have them march around the chairs in the same direction. When you stop the music, each child tries to sit in a chair. The child who is left standing is out. Everyone stands again, and you remove a chair. Play continues until one child is sitting on the last chair.

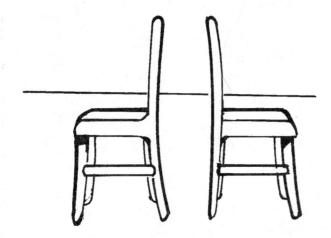

A Tisket, A Tasket

Have the children form a large circle by having them hold hands, step back until their arms are stretched out, and let go. Have the birthday child be "it" and stand outside the circle. Place a handkerchief in her/his hand. Along with the children, recite the rhyme: "A Tisket, a tasket, a green and yellow basket. I wrote a letter to my friend and on the way I dropped it, I dropped it. And on the way I dropped it." As the rhyme is said, the child who is "it" skips around the circle. On the last "I dropped it," the child drops the handkerchief behind another child and runs around the circle. The selected child picks up the handkerchief and chases the child who is "it." The selected child tries to touch the "it" child on the arm or back before he/she gets to the selected child's place. If the child who is "it" gets back to the empty spot without being touched, the selected child is "it" and begins the process again. The game continues until all the children have been "it."

Simon Says

One player, such as the birthday child, is chosen to be "it." That child stands in front of the group and gives a command such as, "Simon says to pat your nose." The children do what Simon says. The leader has to say Simon says for the children to follow the command. If the leader gives a command without saying "Simon says," any child following that command is out. Children who are out can sit down. The winner is the last child left standing. That child then becomes "it" for the next game.

Winners All

By nature, games are competitive, but you need to decide if that's what's important at your party. You can opt to have real winners for many games that are played. Any game that has a score attached to it can have an obvious winner. For other games, this is not so obvious. You will need to decide if having some children win and take home prizes is an important part of the party or if just playing the games is enough.

If you decide there will be distinct winners, then you need to buy prizes and have these ready to give out at the end of each game. You may wish to gift wrap these. It is a good idea to let the birthday child know that while he/she can play every game, he/she is not eligible to be a prize-winner.

There are many ways to make all children into winners. You can give small prizes to everyone for participating. If you choose team games, give each team a different prize. If you have contests, such as hula hoop and dance contests, you can give each child a certificate for something different. Filling out the certificates might take a few minutes so have them ready to go with the children's names on them. Then you or your party helper (page 18) can take a few minutes and write the reason for the award. Make sure that the certificates are given only for positive reasons. If you are at a loss for ideas you can include things like "most original dance" or "most turns of the hula hoop."

Winners All *(cont.)*

The winning team or child can also be the one who gets to be served cake and ice cream first (after the birthday child) or gets to choose where to sit at the table.

If you simply dislike the idea of giving prizes, then don't give any. Choose activities that don't involve any competition, such as making crafts or playing with toys. Party bags at the end of the party are often prize enough for youngsters.

Here is a list of items that make good party prizes. They are small and easy to pass out. Often they come in multiples, so you can buy larger packages and break them apart for distribution.

- stickers
- whistles
- candy
- badges
- hair bands
- pencils
- pens

- plastic animals
- plastic dinosaurs
- crayons
- colored pencils
- socks
- paper leis
- sunglasses

- books
- note pads
- erasers
- rulers
- plastic jewelry
- little cars
- combs

Shortcuts

Even though you'd love to do all of the things described in this book, you know there's not enough time. Below are some shortcuts that might help you to do some of the party ideas on a lesser scale. They are in no particular order and can be used with just about any party.

1. Party bags — Buy colorfully decorated lunch sacks at the grocery store. These are often found next to the plain brown ones. While at the store, buy miniature candies to put in the bags. As a special treat, add stickers or a small book. These can usually be found in the toy aisle. Voila! Your party bags are complete.

2. Choose activities that require little or no set up, especially races and many traditional games. There are many of these described in this book.

3. Serve only cake and ice cream. To make this even simpler, serve cupcakes, ice-cream cups, and juice boxes. This will require only napkins, spoons (which often come with the ice cream cups), and straws (which often come with the juice boxes).

4. Buy helium-filled balloons, and let them serve as decorations. You can keep them in a large bunch where they look very festive, or you can tie one onto each child's chair. At the end of the party untie the balloons and present them as favors.

Note: Make sure you have plenty of extras so everyone gets to take one home.

5. With young children, they are often delighted if you read aloud to them. Choose a good book about a subject that interests your child and the guests. Be sure to read the story to yourself ahead of time. Then read it with lots of expression at the party.

6. Begin a tradition of using a certain type of candles on the cake or special decorations that you can use year after year. For example, if you choose to always have silver candles on the cake, make sure you keep some in the house all year long so you don't even need to think about getting them for the party.

7. Purchase glitter, which is available in small packages or by the scoop at many stationery or party stores. Just putting this out on the table makes everything look festive in the time it takes to sprinkle it.

The Party's Over

The last guest has just left. All of the guests enjoyed themselves, your child was ecstatic about having friends over, and now your house is in shambles. All you want to do is sit down and put your feet up or rush to throw out everything. You look over at your birthday child and see what looks like a long face in the making. You know he/she had a wonderful time, so what's happening? Your youngster is feeling the let down of having the good time end. As a parent you want to make it better. But how? To begin, don't give in to the urge to clean up or sit down. Leaving the decorations up can be helpful, since you can use them to remind your child how much everyone enjoyed them. This would be a good time to talk to your child about the various things that happened during the party.

Review the games that were played and talk about any funny incidents. For example, did someone pin the tail on the teddy bear instead of on the donkey?

What about your child's new gifts? Now might be the perfect time to play with one of these. Card games or board games that you can play together are fun. This is also a good time to give your child a small gift that you have tucked away.

If you took videos of the birthday party, you and your child might enjoy watching them together now.

You can serve a small snack of leftovers from the party. Your child might enjoy a slice of birthday cake and some ice cream. Serve this on party plates if you have any left over. Otherwise, use a special dish or napkin to make it a bit more festive for your child.

Your youngster will soon ease out of the party mode, with lots of happy memories of this special day.

90

Theme Parties

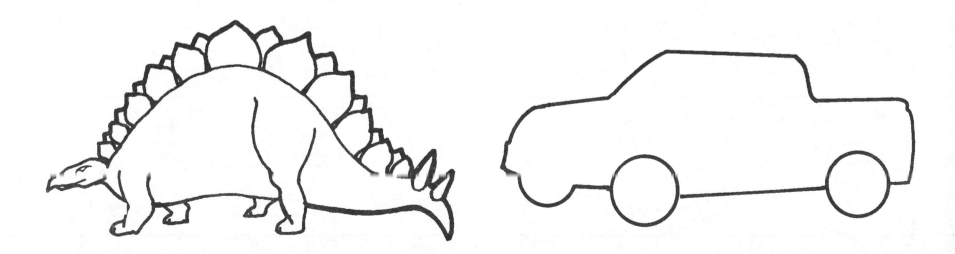

Types of Parties

The types of parties you can have are endless, but your time, energy, and resources aren't. In this section, you will find several types of parties. Each is designed so children can have the most fun, while parents do the least amount of work. Before choosing, carefully weigh all the factors involved, including the wishes of your birthday child. For each party, you should find several or all of the following elements:

- **Invitations:** This section is rich in ideas, templates, and ways you can create or adapt invitations specifics to include on any invitations can be found on page 8.

- **Favors and Prizes:** Here you will find a treasure trove of favor and prize ideas to complement the theme of the party.

- **Table Settings and Decorations:** Look here for inviting and festive ways to set the table for your young party guests.

- **Refreshments:** For the heart of the party — food and beverages that are fun to prepare, eat, and drink — read through this section.

- **Schedule:** This provides a suggested time frame for party events. Use this as a guide to create a schedule that works best for you and your guests.

- **Special:** Many parties have something totally unique to their individual theme. Such elements will range from opening gifts to photo backgrounds.

- **Activities, Games, and Crafts:** This section is chock full of ways to entertain children when they arrive and while they are at the party.

- **Clip Art:** This section includes templates that you can reproduce, trace, or use at the party. Many suggestions for use can be incorporated throughout the party.

Goldie Locks

Baby Bear

Tea Party

This party will be especially appealing to young girls who might wish to wear hats and gloves for a "grown-up" experience.

Invitations

There are many commercial invitations that lend themselves to this kind of party. To create your own invitations, fold heavy pastel paper in half. Place the outline pattern of a teapot (page 96) next to the fold and trace around it. Then cut it out. Let your child decorate the front of the teapot invitations with crayons, markers, clip art, or stickers. You can add the appropriate information (page 8) inside.

Favors and Prizes

Inexpensive teacups and saucers can be purchased at a pottery store. For a special and unusual favor, use a marker designed for writing on pottery to put your child's name and party date on the bottom of each saucer. Send the teacup and saucer home with each girl. Girls of all ages love jewelry and hair accessories. Find some inexpensive necklaces, bracelets, rings, and hair ribbons for terrific favors.

Table Settings and Decorations

Use cloth tablecloths and napkins. A teapot filled with flowers can serve as a centerpiece. Set each place with individual teacups and saucers. (See Favors and Prizes above.)

Refreshments

Serve lemonade and/or hot chocolate, cookies, tea cakes, petit fours (little pastries iced in pastel colors), and sandwiches with the crusts cut off. Use cookie cutters to make the sandwiches into fancy and/or funny shapes. As an alternative to having a birthday cake, put the candles into the tea cakes or petit fours.

Tea Party (cont.)

Schedule

20–25 minutes	Children arrive. They make cookies.
15–20 minutes	Make hats.
15–30 minutes	Play games.
15–20 minutes	Open gifts.
20–30 minutes	Serve refreshments.
5–15 minutes	Model hats and fancy clothes.

As the guests arrive, let them help bake cookies for the party. Use a simple recipe or a commercial cut-and-bake dough. Have aprons ready or use some old shirts as smocks so the party clothes won't be soiled. Add sprinkles or other shake-on decorations. Make sure you have extra cookies already baked and ready to serve in case there's an unforeseen problem, such as some cookies being burned.

Special

On the invitation, tell partygoers to dress up in fancy clothes. Invite parents to come back about 10 minutes before the end of the party. When they return, have an impromptu fashion show in which the children model their hats and fancy clothes.

Activities, Games, and Crafts

Making Hats

You will need paper plates, paper bowls, masking tape, glitter, glue, feathers, sequins, markers, crayons, hole punch, and ribbon. Each child cuts out the center of a paper plate and tapes a bowl inside it. (**Note:** For younger children, consider having this done before the party begins.) The paper plate becomes the hat brim. Have the children decorate it using assorted materials. On opposite sides of the hat brim, punch one hole and thread a piece of ribbon through each so the hat can be tied under the child's chin. Have the children wear their hats to the table when the refreshments are served.

94

Tea Party (cont.)

Activities, Games, and Crafts (cont.)

Stack the Teacups

In a novelty store, buy inexpensive plastic cups and saucers. Divide the children evenly into two teams. Set one section of each team at opposite ends of a room. (**Note:** Put younger children a few feet apart.) Have the first member of each team take a cup and saucer and run to the other half of the team. A second member takes that cup and saucer, adds another set on top, and runs to the first half of the team. When the cups and saucers fall, have the child restack them and continue. Be sure each team member has a turn. Variations include making teams start over when the cups and saucers fall, having everyone on one team, or having each child go two or three times if there are only a few guests.

Opening Presents

You might consider having each child model his or her hat then sit next to the birthday child as her present is opened. This gives the present-giver a moment in the limelight with the birthday child. Consider taking a picture of each guest with your child. These make a great addition to the thank-you notes.

The Tea Party

Have the children come to the table after the presents are opened. Offer lemonade and hot chocolate from teapots and serve their cookies. If you decided to give teacups and saucers as favors, have them drink from those. (**Note:** You will have to wash them before sending them home.) If you're serving lunch, quartered cucumber sandwiches without crusts make a nice treat. Then bring in the cake and sing "Happy Birthday."

Drop the Teabag

This is a variation of Drop the Clothespins in the Bottle (page 83). Each child is given five teabags and tries to drop them into a (metal) teapot or tea kettle.

Tea Party *(cont.)*

Clip Art

Flowers

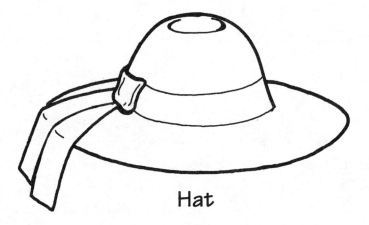

Hat

Teabag

Teapot

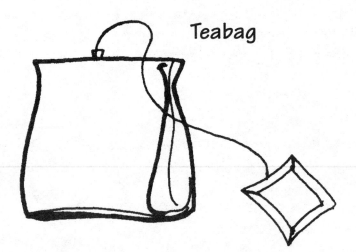

Cars and Trucks Party

This party will appeal to young children, especially boys, who will enjoy bringing their own favorite toys to the festivities. If you're looking for a party that will appeal to two- and three-year-olds, who might not be ready to join in large group activities, this could be just the ticket.

Invitations

Your youngster will have fun stamping pictures of cars and/or trucks on the invitations. There is usually a great selection at any place where rubber stamps are sold. Find some simple invitations with plenty of white space on them, and let the stamping begin.

Favors and Prizes

This should be an easy one — toy cars and trucks. Shop around until you find those in your price range. If you have very small cars and trucks, make sure they aren't so small that they might cause a problem if youngsters put them in their mouths. To avoid squabbles among the guests, you might give every partygoer the same car or truck (in the same color).

Table Settings and Decorations

Your child probably has quite a collection of toy cars and trucks that you could use as decorations. As long as you ask the guests to please leave the decorations where they are, you can make your table into a mini-Indianapolis 500 or a highway. A white paper tablecloth can easily be made to look like a racing oval or freeway by using markers to draw roads on it. Then add the appropriate cars and/or trucks.

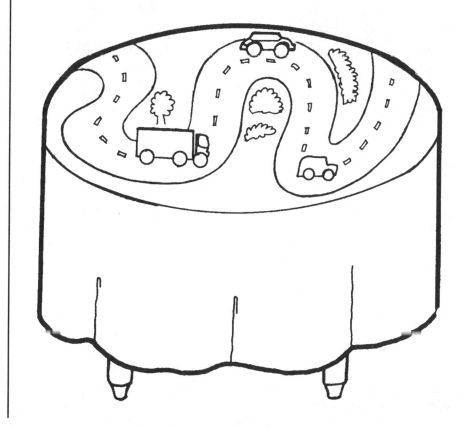

Refreshments

What does your youngster like to eat? That's what you should have, for more than likely this is what the guests will also enjoy. Truckers usually eat good old American fare — hamburgers, chili, and fries. Visit a local truck stop and let your birthday child see what foods look good. A local market will have a variety of cakes with car and truck themes. Some might have removable toy cars and trucks the children can save. If not, buy some small ones and add these to the top of each cake portion. While you might not want to serve the trucker's trusty mug of coffee, it might be fun to serve soda or hot chocolate in mugs for those truckin' tots.

Schedule

20–30 minutes	Children arrive. Decorate "car" boxes.
20–30 minutes	Play games.
15–30 minutes	Serve refreshments.
10–20 minutes	Open gifts.
15–30 minutes	Have free play with cars and trucks.

Special

As a special treat, let the children make cars to wear! You will need boxes large enough for the kids to fit into with some extra room. Before the guests arrive, cut off the bottoms of the boxes and the flaps from the top. Poke two holes on opposite sides of each box. Tie heavy cord to these holes for the straps. The straps should fit comfortably on the driver's shoulders. Provide construction paper, scissors, glue, and markers. Let the children decorate their cars. You can also enlarge and reproduce the clip art (page 100) for the children to use. (**Note:** For the younger crowd, have everything pre-cut and invite them to glue on the clip art or draw the parts that they want on their cars.) During game time have the children race their cars. You can create a track outside using chalk or inside by placing masking tape on the ground. Depending on the area, give the okay to run the race!

Activities, Games, and Crafts

Car and Truck Races

If you encourage the guests to bring their own toys, make sure they are clearly labeled with tape that will stick as long as the party lasts. Take a long plank of wood, at least 9 inches (23 cm) wide and 5–6 feet (1.5–1.8 m) long. Prop one end up on a low stool. Have the guests position their cars and/or trucks at the highest point of the plank and then let them go. Mark where each toy stops or falls off. You might give each child two or three chances.

Find-the-Truck

This is a hide-and-go-seek game, but only a toy truck is hidden. Determine which room of your house is most childproof. Gather the guests in another room while you hide the truck. If you have any items in the room you don't want touched, don't hide the truck anywhere near those spots. Set the ground rules about where the children can and cannot look. Then give them one minute to find the hidden truck.

Free Play

Little ones might be happiest with about half an hour of free play. Monitor their activity and let them enjoy themselves. You might find it great fun to listen to the games they make up. It often beats anything you can create for them. This will allow the children to either play with each other or alone. This might seem like a cop-out to those who feel that a party must be planned to the last second. However, little ones often have the best time left to their own devices.

Cars and Trucks Party *(cont.)*

Clip Art

Wheels

Headlights

Steering Wheel

Truck

Hat

KEEP ON TRUCKIN'

Car

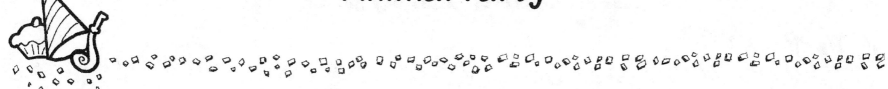

Animal Party

This party is for animal lovers. Children like to pretend to be animals. They all have their favorite animals and enjoy creating animal figures and crafts. This party has it all.

Invitations

You can create invitations by using the clip art on page 104. Write the party information (page 8) at the bottom of an 8½" x 11" (22 cm x 28 cm) piece of paper. Reproduce or trace one of the animals on page 104 and have your child color it. Cut it out and glue it to the paper. Tracing around animal-shaped cookie cutters is another easy way for children to help make the invitations. Many computer programs also have animal clip art that can be incorporated into the invitations.

Favors and Prizes

You can find lots of animal stickers to give to children. Other favors that are appropriate to an animal theme include tiny stuffed animals, plastic animal figurines, and other items that have animals on them. If you are fortunate enough to live near a zoo, animal park, aquarium, or natural history museum, there are usually lots of inexpensive items available at the gift shops that would make a special treat. A box of animal crackers is also an appropriate favor or prize.

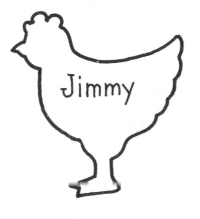

Table Settings and Decorations

Encourage children to bring their own small stuffed animals. Make sure they are clearly labeled with tape. Arrange them in a basket to serve as a centerpiece. If you prefer, let your child choose a favorite stuffed or plastic animal for the table centerpiece. Individual stuffed animals at each place can also be an attractive table decoration.

Refreshments

There are a few options as to what to serve your guests. One is to serve them the foods that animals might eat. While, of course, you wouldn't serve dog food, you might serve cookies cut to look like dog bones or bananas like monkeys would eat.

Schedule

15–20 minutes	Children arrive. Play with clay.
20–30 minutes	Play games.
15–30 minutes	Serve refreshments.
10–20 minutes	Open gifts.
15–20 minutes	Do Follow the Footprints and Create an Animal.

Special

Having live animals is not a good idea at a party. Someone might be scared, another person might be allergic, or the animal might get out of control. You can, however, have some special things about animals. You can set up a table with various items that belong to unusual animals and matching pictures. Children can look at and try to guess which animal the object belongs to. For instance, you can find duck feathers, a snakeskin, and dog hair and place each in a plastic bag for display.

Have the children play with clay or playdough (page 77) when they arrive. Encourage them to create animals and their habitats, such as birds in nests or bears in caves. They can set these on the table to help decorate it and mark their places.

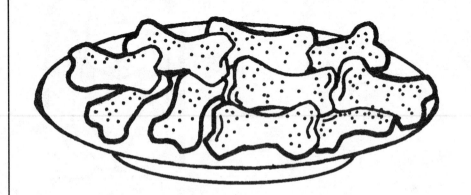

Animal Party *(cont.)*

Activities, Games, and Crafts

Animal Charades or Who Am I?

Write different animal names on slips of paper. Place the slips in a hat or bag. Each child takes a turn and picks a slip. The child has to act like the animal as the other children guess what she/he is.

Animal Races

Ducks waddle, horses gallop, and crabs do a kind of crawl. Choose lots of different types of animals. Ask the children to race in the way that the animals would move. You can do this in teams or as individuals. Just set the distance far enough so children can move around and have fun at the same time. Other animals to include are kangaroos, frogs, flamingos (on one leg), lions, birds, snakes, and monkeys.

Follow the Footprints

Pick three or four different animal footprints (page 104). Place them on the floor. Have children choose the prints they wish to follow. They can only follow the footprints of the animal they have chosen. They should ignore the others. The footprints can lead to the table where they will create their animals for the final activity.

Create an Animal

Give children lots of craft materials, such as feathers, sequins, scraps of fabric, paper towel tubes, margarine tubs, scissors, glue, paper, crayons, and a stapler. Let them create a mixed-up animal. Have each child name her/his animal. Then see if the other children can guess the various animals whose characteristics went into making this new one.

Animal Party (cont.)

Clip Art

Chicken

Dog

Horse

Cat

Cow

Pig

Under the Sea Party

Children find the ocean and its inhabitants fascinating. If you have a child who is fascinated with the beach or sea life, this will be the perfect birthday party.

Invitations

Create invitations in the shape of a fish or use the clip art on page 108 to put on the front of an invitation. You can add a small sprinkle of sand in each invitation so children can anticipate the party when they open the envelopes.

You are Invited!

Favors and Prizes

Seashells are wonderful favors for children to take home from a party. Little ones especially love the big conch shells that they can hold up to their ears and listen to the ocean. There are also large shells that can be filled with smaller shells and then covered with plastic wrap. Many gift shops sell seashells. There are also some available from catalogs. Buying the seashells is a good idea because they will be clean and dry.

Fish stickers, books about the ocean or sea animals, fish-shaped barrettes, combs in the shape of fish, and small plastic sea creatures make good favors.

Table Settings and Decorations

Start with a bright blue tablecloth to represent the ocean. Decorate it with shells, gummy worms, and goldfish crackers. If you have some fish bowls or a small aquarium, you might share some of your watery pets with the partygoers.

Refreshments

If you're serving food, you might try some tuna sandwiches. Make sure you have goldfish crackers, too. Add a few drops of blue food coloring to lemon-lime soda and serve the beverages in clear plastic glasses. You may be able to find plastic, water-fill fish that you can freeze for ice cubes.

Under the Sea Party *(cont.)*

Schedule

15–20 minutes	Children arrive. Create shell collages.
15–25 minutes	Dig for shells. Make sandcastles.
15–20 minutes	Serve refreshments.
10–20 minutes	Open gifts.
15–20 minutes	Play Going Fishing.

Activities, Games, and Crafts

Shell Collages

Using white glue, cardboard, and tiny real shells or shell clip art (page 108) have children create collages. Before gluing the shells, have them outline what they want the shells to cover. They can also add bits of undersea greenery to their pictures and tiny precut fish.

Sea Creatures

Let the children select shells and decide how to use them to make sea creatures. Have an adult use a hot glue gun to put the creatures together. Once a dot of glue is on a shell, let the child stick two shells together, holding them in place for a few seconds. Provide wiggly eyes and pipe cleaners to add to the sea creatures.

Sandcastles

Why not build sandcastles at your party? If you do not live near the beach, you will need to provide lots of sand. The obvious place to put it is in a sandbox or plastic wading pool. Think carefully before you decide to do this, since sand can cause children to slip and is difficult to get rid of. However, if you decide to proceed, provide buckets, shovels, spoons, water, watering cans, icing spreaders, and any other tool that will allow children to create fanciful castles.

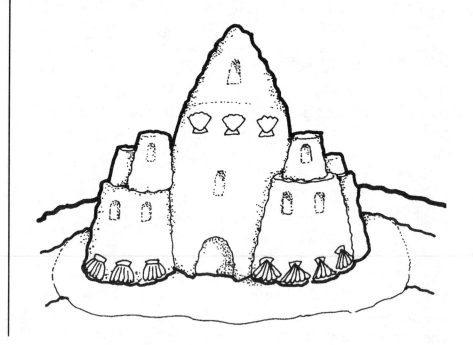

Activities, Games, and Crafts *(cont.)*

Dig for Shells

If you have access to a sandbox, place several seashells in it. Then let the children use a sieve or colander to sift through the sand and collect the seashells.

Going Fishing

This takes a little organization before the party. However, the results and the looks on the children's faces make it worthwhile. You need a fishing booth for you or your party helper (page 18) to hide in or behind. Use a blanket draped over a large appliance box, a table, some chairs, or the side of a staircase. Decide which small, lightweight gifts you want the children to "fish" for. Sea life stickers or coloring books about the ocean work well. Gift wrap these to make them more special.

Make a fishing pole from a lightweight dowel with fishing line attached to one end and a clamp or movable clothespin attached to the other. You can tie or staple the clamp or clothespin onto the line. Before the party, use it a few times to be sure the line is secure. (**Note:** Making more than one pole is a good idea.) Let the children take turns fishing. Have them practice throwing out the line. Once they throw it into the fishing booth, the person there can tug on the line a few times.

Occasionally throw it back over without anything attached. Of course, give that child the opportunity to try again. Attach the "fish" to the line so the child gets a gift.

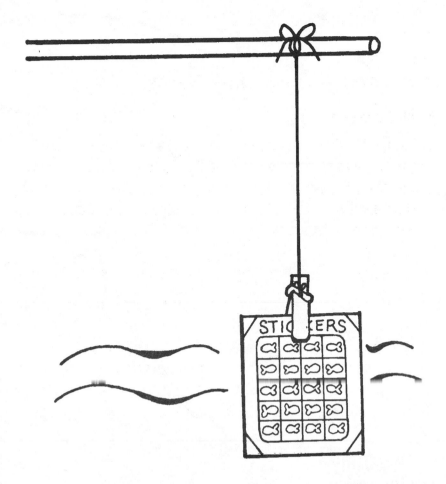

Clip Art

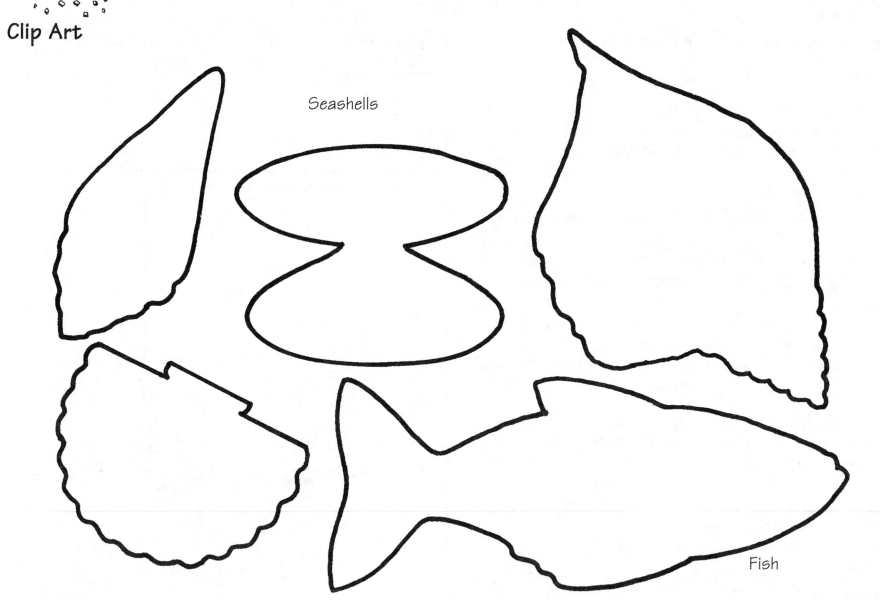

Seashells

Fish

Good Morning Pajama Party

Since young children often wake up early, have this party in the morning and serve breakfast!

Invitations

Make a sunny-side-up egg using a large white circle with a smaller yellow circle glued to the inside. Write the party information (page 8) on the middle of the "egg." Reproduce and cut out the bacon clip art (page 112). Glue it onto the white part of the egg.

Favors and Prizes

Inexpensive plastic mugs and bowls used at the table can make fun keepsakes. Set the table with them and then wash them before the children take them home. The brighter the colors, the better.

Prizes for this party can include small boxes of cereal and food stickers, especially those that are the scratch-and-sniff type.

Table Settings and Decorations

Before the children come, wrap up the forks and spoons with festive napkins, each tied loosely with a ribbon. Let children create their own placemats (page 110). Then place the bowls, mugs, wrapped utensils, and other dishes on the placemats.

Decorations for this party can be various breakfast foods or boxes. A collage on a few pieces of poster board can be quite a lot of fun for you and your child to create before the party.

Good Morning Pajama Party *(cont.)*

Refreshments

Breakfast foods mean different things depending on your child, the guests, and how much preparation you want to do. Cereal and milk are easy and can be made special using little boxes of cereal and individual cartons of milk. Mini-muffins or mini-donuts make a special treat. You can also serve the traditional bacon and eggs or pigs in a blanket, which are pancakes rolled around sausages. Waffles with different flavored syrups are sure to please. Juice boxes or mugs of hot chocolate are also an option. A cake for this party might be a coffee cake or a cinnamon bun with candles in it. Ask your child what he/she prefers.

Schedule

15–30 minutes	Children arrive. Create placemats.
15–30 minutes	The Pancake Race and Cereal Box Stack.
15–30 minutes	Serve breakfast. Play "What did I eat for breakfast?"
10–20 minutes	Open gifts.
15–20 minutes	Have pajama fashion show.

Special

Little children love the opportunity to wear their pajamas anywhere. Why not have them come to the party wearing them? You can even have a pajama fashion show.

Activities, Games, and Crafts

Placemats

Give the children plain colored placemats. Write their names on the placemats. Let the children use markers and crayons to decorate the placemats. When they finish, collect the placemats and put them at the table where you want the children to sit. An alternative is to cover the table with white butcher paper and draw lines to divide it into sections. Label each section with a child's name. Have the children color their designated sections. The sections can also be used to seat them at the table. If you prefer, have the children color the butcher paper wherever they wish.

Good Morning Pajama Party *(cont.)*

Activities, Games, and Crafts *(cont.)*

Pancake Race

To play this game, you will need some ready-made pancakes, paper plates, and pancake turners for each team.

(**Note:** Microwavable pancakes work fine for this.) Put the children into two or three teams. Next to the first person in line for each team, place a plate with one pancake for each child on the team. The first person is given a pancake turner. You place a pancake on the pancake turner. Once you say "Go," the first racer has to try to flip the pancake while moving as quickly as possible to the halfway point. Once there, the child turns around and comes back, still trying to flip the pancake. The child

has to stop and put the pancake back on the turner if it drops. When this racer returns to the team, he/she hands off the pancake turner but not the pancake. The next team member takes a new pancake from the plate and does the same thing. The race continues until all of the children have had a turn. Make sure you have extra pancakes on hand to replace those that fall apart. If you are doing this with very young children, skip the flipping part.

Cereal Box Stack

How many small boxes of cereal can the children stack before they all fall over? Gather at least 30 boxes of cereal. Have the children take turns stacking the boxes to see how many they can pile up before the boxes fall down.

What Did I Eat for Breakfast?

This is a good word game to play at the table while children are waiting to eat. Start with the birthday child who says, "Yesterday I ate three eggs for breakfast." The next child says, "Yesterday I ate two bowls of cereal and three eggs for breakfast." Play continues until children can no longer remember the list of breakfast foods or it is time for you to serve breakfast.

Good Morning Pajama Party (cont.)

Clip Art

Bacon

Bowl of Cereal

HOMOGENIZED

MILK

Eggs

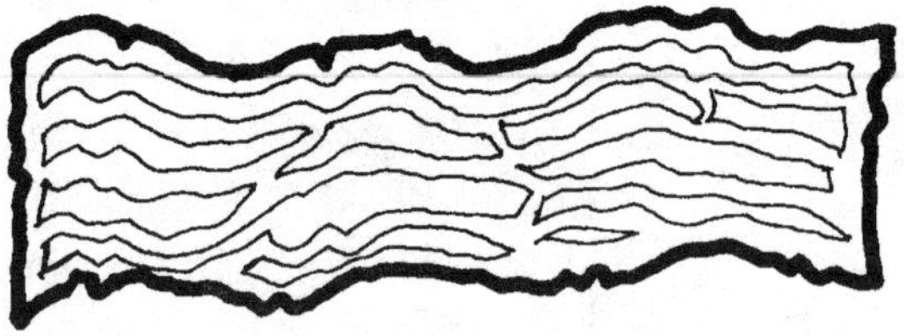

Milk

Circus and Clowns Party

Circus, clowns, and children seem to blend well together as the birthday child celebrates with lots of laughter and circus tricks.

Invitations

Reproduce the big top circus tent (page 117). Cut along the bottom and sides of the flap on the tent and fold it up. Glue the tent onto another piece of paper making sure you don't glue down the flap. Write the invitation information (page 8) under the flap. Shut the flap. On the outside write something like "Look inside the tent for an invitation to Elise's birthday party." You might want to place these invitations in large envelopes.

Favors and Prizes

This type of party lends itself to anything having to do with the circus. Balloons, whistles, and magic tricks that children can easily do are fun favors and prizes. Silly glasses and noses, small boxes of animal crackers, and big round lollipops are also appropriate prizes. You can often find clown noses that slip over children's noses or squirting flowers such as a clown might use. Many times you can buy cotton candy in plastic sacks or peanuts in circus bags. (**Warning:** Make sure no one is allergic to peanuts.)

Table Settings and Decorations

Bright colors and balloons are the order of the day. Big balloon bouquets are fine and so are balloons on sticks. Place them in a vase on the table and give them out as favors. Use the big round lollipops as table decorations. Place an inverted paper cup at each place. Poke the lollipop through it. Not only does it look decorative, but it also makes a good favor. Use stripes on the table and on the wall. Hang small banners at the door like those displayed at the circus. You might want to hang an old sheet or piece of canvas on the top of the door to create a flap. Put a sign on it that says "Welcome to the Circus." Push it aside as the children enter.

Refreshments

Have bowls of animal crackers for the children to nibble on. This party lends itself to serving sweets since you might want to replicate what children would eat at a circus. This could include peanuts, caramel coated popcorn, cotton candy, snow cones, and candied apples, to name a few. For something more substantial, hamburgers and hot dogs are most appropriate. The cake can be decorated with plastic circus figurines or with balloons made from icing. You can also serve ice-cream cone clowns. These can be bought at some ice-cream stores. If you want to make your own, place a scoop of ice cream on a plate and then put a sugar cone on top. Put this back in the freezer to harden. Use tubes of store-bought icing in various colors to create a face. For an extra touch, put a small doily on the plate first to create a clown collar.

Schedule

10–15 minutes	Children arrive. Conduct Peanut Races.
15–20 minutes	Make clown hats.
20–30 minutes	Become clowns.
15–20 minutes	Serve refreshments.
10–15 minutes	Open gifts.
15–20 minutes	Choose from other activities.

Special

You might want to hire a clown for this party. If you do, check your local yellow pages or ask friends for recommendations. Keep in mind this could be expensive. When the clown arrives, don't be surprised if some of the children are frightened. If this is the case, respect their fear and don't force them to be involved with the clown. A clown with experience will understand.

Circus and Clowns Party *(cont.)*

Activities, Games, and Crafts

Clowns

Before the party, be sure to inform parents that you are planning a face-painting activity so they don't dress the children in their best clothes. Get some special white face paint. This is often available in costume, craft, or toy stores. Follow the directions for the children to paint their faces. You can also make face paints. For each color, use 1 tablespoon (15 mL) of cold cream, 1 tablespoon (15 mL) of water, 2 tablespoons (30 mL) of cornstarch, and a few drops of food coloring. Use a plastic spoon to stir these together in a cup. Apply the paint with sponges or brushes. **Avoid the eye area.** The cold cream is easy to wash off. Have plenty of paper towels for both washing and drying. Then provide slip-on red clown noses or let the children paint red dots on the end of their noses. Provide oversized jackets, hats, and shoes. Have the children create their outfits and perform tricks, such as trying to juggle bean bags or balance balls on their noses.

Peanut Races

The children will shriek with delight during these races. This is best done as a relay with four children on each team. Line them up in sets of two on different sides of the race area. Place a peanut on the floor for each team. When you say "Go," the first child uses her/his nose to push the peanut to the other side. The child on the other side brings it back. This continues until everyone has gone.

Clown Hats

Most children probably think of a tall cone-shaped hat as a clown hat. Provide each child with this type of hat. Either roll paper into a cone shape and add ribbon to each side so it can be tied under the chin or buy plain ready-made hats at a party supply store. Let the children glue glitter, bits of fabric, clown poems, and sequins onto the hats. The children can wear the hats to the table and then take them home.

Activities, Games, and Crafts *(cont.)*

Pin the Nose on the Clown

This variation of Pin the Tail on the Donkey (page 82) requires a large picture of a clown and lots of round, red noses cut from construction paper. You can enlarge the picture of the clown on page 117 and create noses to fit.

Three Ring Circus

Circus acts often take place in three rings. Make three rings using hula hoops or masking tape circles. Then invite three children into the rings to perform in the circus. In one ring, have the first child imitate a circus animal of your choice. For instance, the child could be a seal that juggles a ball on its nose. In another ring, invite a second child to be a clown. Have that child run around in the circle or turn around and get people to clap. In the last ring, have a child try to do a circus trick. The trick might be to juggle lots of balls in the air or balance a spinning plate on a long stick. Use a beach ball for the seal, bean bags or peacock feathers for the juggler, and a long thin dowel and a Frisbee for the spinning plate. Let the performers practice for a while. They may be surprised how difficult these are to do, especially with others performing different things at the same time.

Circus Figures

Using clay (page 77), have children make circus animals. Let them create whichever ones they wish. You can open a box of animal crackers and let them use these as models if they can't think of any circus animals to make. You might even suggest they all make elephants and then place a parade of elephants on the table.

Clip Art

Circus Tent

Clown

-Fold-   -Fold-

Elephants

Pirate Party

There's something about pirates that makes children expect a fun time. This party will be one your child will always remember.

Invitations

Use the pirate ship (page 122) for the invitations. Write the pertinent information (page 8) on the sail. On the bottom you can write, "Ahoy, Mate! Take the ship to Roger's Birthday." You might have your child draw a self-portrait on the flag instead of the traditional skull and crossbones.

Favors and Prizes

Give each child a treasure to take home. Find some small tin boxes with lids. Fill these with seashells. Hidden among the shells put in some chocolate coins that are covered with gold foil, pennies, and a gift certificate for an ice cream cone or hamburger. Inexpensive bandannas that can be tied on also make fun favors.

Table Settings and Decorations

Put a treasure map on the front door. Make the map yourself on a large sheet of butcher paper. Place a large X where the birthday cake goes. When the time comes for cake to be served, bring the children back to the treasure map and let them try to figure out where the cake is. You can also add long strings to the map and let the children follow the strings from the map to the table. Set the table with a large pile of gold coins in the middle and strings of plastic beads. You can make the coins by wrapping real coins, checkers, or any other disk-shaped objects with gold foil. You can also get chocolate coins that are covered with gold foil.

Refreshments

Have a pirate cake. This can be a cake with a plastic pirate ship on it or lots of buried treasure in the form of gold and silver wrapped coins. These coins should be standing up on their edges.

Pirate Party *(cont.)*

Schedule

15–25 minutes	Children arrive. Make pirate hats and eye patches.
15–20 minutes	Guess the treasure.
15–20 minutes	Paint sand.
15–20 minutes	Serve refreshments. Play the Polly Parrot game.
10–15 minutes	Open gifts.
15–20 minutes	Have a treasure hunt.

Special

You may want to show the *Peter Pan* video by Walt Disney (Buena Vista Home Video). This cartoon includes Captain Hook and his band of pirates. Let the children watch it while nibbling on some treats of their choice.

Activities, Games, and Crafts

Pirate Hats and Eye Patches

Make the newspaper hats found on page 52. Provide black, red, and white markers to decorate them. Give each child a feather to tape onto the side of his or her pirate hat. If you can't find feathers, cut up a few new, brightly colored feather dusters from the store.

To make eye patches, you will need black construction paper cut into circles large enough to cover a child's eye. With a hole punch, make two holes on either side of the patch. Let the children decorate the eye patches. White-out pens make good tools with which to decorate. Once the ink is dry, thread yarn through the two holes and tie the patches around the children's heads.

Have children wear the hats and eye patches for pictures, but don't expect them to wear them much longer than that.

Pirate Party *(cont.)*

Activities, Games, and Crafts *(cont.)*

Treasure Hunt

Decide first what the treasure will be and where you will hide it. If you have a large hiding place, you could take all the presents the children bring and hide them in a closet or behind a piece of furniture. A smaller treasure might be gold coins, one for each guest, hidden in a large coffee can. This would work well if you can have your treasure hunt outside. Whatever you hide, make sure it cannot be found without using the clues you provide. Have enough clues so that each partygoer can figure one out. Use drawings instead of words since your little ones probably can't read yet. You'll need to have adults ready to answer questions, but don't tell them where the treasure is. Let them join the fun with the youngsters. For the first clue, you could draw two chairs that are placed together. When the children find the two chairs, the second clue can be taped onto the bottom of one of them. The second clue might show a drawing of a wagon in the backyard. Depending on the children's ages, make the next clue in the series easier or harder to find. If you have neighbors who want to be part of the game, you can stretch this out along your block. (**Note:** You might want to try this game with your birthday child a couple weeks before the party to make sure the trail is not too difficult to follow.)

Polly Parrot Says

A parrot is often associated with pirates, so play this word game with children. You need to start the sentence so children can rhyme something with the words you give them. Have children rhyme words and then see if they can remember everyone else's rhyme. With very young children, coming up with the rhymes are probably enough. Say, "Polly Parrot says she likes red bread. Polly says she also likes nice _____." The child has to fill in the blank. Some good words for rhyming are *hat, house, bee, toy, sit, fun,* and *park.*

Activities, Games, and Crafts *(cont.)*

Sand Painting

Pirates often have to go on shore where there is lots of sand. Do some sand painting with the children. Before the party, you'll need to do some preparation. For each child, reproduce the pirate ship (page 122) on heavy paper or cut a piece of poster board. You can buy commercially prepared sand in a craft store, or you can make your own. (**Note:** Salt is a good substitute for real sand.) Pour some sand into several resealable plastic bags and add a few drops of food coloring to each. Seal the bags and shake them until the color mixes evenly in the sand. Open the bags and let the sand dry for a couple of hours.

During the party explain to the children how to spread the glue and sprinkle one color of sand onto an area of the picture or poster board. Allow the glue to dry. Then gently shake off any extra sand. Have them repeat this procedure using the different colors of sand until their pictures are complete.

Guess the Treasure

Place an interesting object in a large decorated box or a pirate hat (page 119), hiding it from view. This could be a plastic shovel, seashell, coconut, or something else associated with ships, deserted islands, or treasures. Have several items ready for the game. Give clues about the hidden object until a partygoer guesses it correctly. Have someone take the box or hat into another room, quickly place the next item in it, and return. (**Note:** If older children are playing, instead of giving clues have them ask questions that pertain to shape, color, or texture.) Tell the children they can only guess what the object is by saying, "Ahoy, I'm ready to tell what is in 'yar' hat (box)." Recognize that child and have her/him guess. Anyone who guesses incorrectly must walk the plank. Make the plank from a board that is about 10 feet (3 m) long and 1 foot (0.3 m) wide. Place some bricks or books at either end of the plank so that it is about 4 inches (10 cm) above the ground. You might blindfold older children — just make sure that they can't get hurt if they fall.

Clip Art

Pirate Ship

Fairy Tale Party

This is where your partygoers come as their favorite fairy tale characters. This is definitely a winner with those who have worn out their Disney videos!

Invitations

Enlarge and reproduce the castle pattern (page 133) for the invitations. Cut the top and sides of the castle door. Glue the castle onto another piece of paper, making sure you do not glue down the door. Place the information about the party (page 8) under the castle door. When children receive the invitation, they fold down the castle door and feel like the party has already begun.

Favors and Prizes

Inexpensive fairy tale books are wonderful favors and prizes for the children to take home. You can also give out magic wands, garlands, pakets of fairy dust (glitter), or crowns.

Table Settings and Decorations

A stack of fairy tale books makes a beautiful centerpiece, especially if they are opened to some lovely pages of art. Also any figurines, dolls, or stuffed fairy tale characters can be grouped alone or with the books. Crowns and fairy wands are quite magical when set together on the table. Small plastic fairy tale figures can be used to decorate the cake or individual places. A crown is also a good cake decoration. You may wish to spread "fairy dust," otherwise known as glitter, on the table. Depending on how much you want to clean up afterwards, fairy dust can also be sprinkled near the front door to welcome the children as they enter the house.

Refreshments

Serve traditional birthday fare and pink lemonade. Use cookie cutters to cut sandwiches into whimsical shapes.

Fairy Tale Party *(cont.)*

Schedule

20–25 minutes	Children arrive. Make puppets.
15–25 minutes	Practice the puppet show.
15–20 minutes	Serve refreshments.
10–20 minutes	Open gifts.
15–20 minutes	Share a story. Make up fairy tales.
15–20 minutes	Present the puppet show.

Special

Invite parents to come watch the puppet show. Make sure you tell them that this is part of the party. They will be entertained for about 15 minutes or so when they come to pick up their children.

Activities, Games, and Crafts

Making Puppets

Have the children make stick puppets. Reproduce the patterns (pages 132 and 133) onto index paper. Depending on the age of the children, you may need to pre-cut the puppets. Provide crayons, glue or tape, and craft sticks. Have the children choose the characters they like best. If a character isn't chosen, you or your party helper (page 18) can put that puppet together or make a set of puppets in advance. You can easily have more than one of each character. Just group the same character puppets together. Let the children color their puppets and attach them to the craft sticks. Make sure each child's name or initials is on the back of the puppet. As you read each story (pages 127–131), encourage the children to move their puppets.

Fairy Tale Party (cont.)

Activities, Games, and Crafts (cont.)

Puppet Show

At the end of the party, present a puppet show to parents using one or both of the stories in this book (pages 127–131). Create a makeshift puppet stage by draping a blanket or sheet over the backs of two sturdy chairs. Hide the children behind the chairs with only their stick-puppets visible to the audience. You don't really need a background or too much movement. The stories have been written so they are easy to do, while being entertaining for the children and the parent audience. An adult should narrate the story so it moves swiftly. Before the show, be sure to read the story to the children and demonstrate how each puppet needs to move. Tell them to move their stick puppets just a little, up and down or side to side, as the narrator reads the dialog. One full practice with the children is usually enough. If some mistakes are made during the performance, the parents will enjoy it even more. At the end of the performance, have the puppeteers bow while holding their puppets.

Costumes

Children should be encouraged to wear costumes to this party. They do not need to buy or rent them. Most children have costumes of fairy tale characters that they have made, or they may have costumes they used for Halloween. The wearing of costumes shouldn't be a requirement, but it will make this party more colorful as well as more exciting. Make sure you have plenty of film.

Fairy Tale Party *(cont.)*

Read a Fairy Tale

If your child has a favorite fairy tale, she/he probably would enjoy sharing it with the guests. Your child can help read it or show the pictures as you read it.

Make Up a Fairy Tale

Older children might enjoy making up their own fairy tale. Seat the children in a circle. (**Note:** You might want to have a tape recorder handy.) An adult begins. For example the adult might say, "Once upon a time, a boy named Charles and his sister named Nicole were walking through the forest. They were on their way to visit their grandmother when a deer walked up to them. The deer said, _____."

Have the birthday child add the next sentence or two. (**Note:** You may wish to rehearse this with your child ahead of time.) Your child might continue the story by saying, "Children, it will be getting dark soon, and you shouldn't be in the woods alone. I think you should come to my house." Charles said, "I don't want to come with you." Nicole said, "We must go to our grandmother's house." They continued to walk when _____.

Have the next child in the circle add to the story. This usually is an enjoyable game for children, and what they come up with may amaze the parents in the room.

Fairy Tale Party *(cont.)*

Goldilocks and the Three Bears

Once upon a time three bears sat in their house in the woods. They were eating porridge. Papa Bear said, "This is too hot. We should go for a walk and let the porridge cool down." Mama Bear said, "Yes, I think you're right. Let's go right now." Baby Bear said, "Right now." And off they went.

A little girl named Goldilocks was also going for a walk in the woods. She was carrying a basket and singing to herself. "La-la-la-la." She came to the bears' house and saw the door was open. She walked right in, even though her mother had told her many times never to go into a stranger's house. She set down her basket and looked around. She saw the porridge and tasted some from Papa Bear's big bowl. "Oh, this is too hot." She tried some from Mama Bear's medium bowl. "Yuck, this is too cold." She tasted a bit from Baby Bear's little bowl. "Yum, this is perfect," and she ate it all.

Next she spied some chairs and decided to sit down. First she sat in Papa Bear's big one. "Ouch, this is too hard." Then she moved to Mama Bear's middle-sized chair and said, "Oooh, this is too soft." Finally, she tried Baby Bear's little one. "Ah, this is so comfortable." She began to rock the chair. Then all of a sudden she heard a cracking noise. However, before she could get up, the chair broke into a hundred pieces and Goldilocks was sitting on the floor. "Oh dear, that chair wasn't very strong. I think I need to lie down after such a frightening

Goldilocks walked upstairs to the bedroom. First, of course, she tried Papa Bear's big bed. "Heavens, this is hard as a rock." Next she went to Mama Bear's medium-sized bed. "My goodness, this is as soft as a wet noodle." Then she cautiously moved to Baby Bear's little bed. "I know this one will be just right, but I hope it can hold me." It was perfect, and it did hold her. Goldilocks fell fast asleep.

Goldilocks and the Three Bears *(cont.)*

After a while, the three bears returned home from their walk. "That walk was just what we needed," said Papa Bear. "Yes, it was a fine walk," added Mama Bear. "A fine walk," Baby Bear agreed. They went to their table. "I think someone has been eating my porridge," roared Papa Bear. "Yes, and someone has tasted my porridge," added Mama Bear. "Tasted my porridge," Baby Bear agreed, "and ate it all up." They quickly got up from the table and went into the living room. "I think someone has been sitting in my chair," roared Papa Bear. "Yes, I think someone has been sitting in my chair, too," added Mama Bear. "Sitting in my chair," cried Baby Bear, "and it is broken into a hundred pieces." Papa Bear was trying to figure this out when he heard some noises from upstairs. He wasted no time in climbing the stairs, followed by Mama Bear and Baby Bear. "Someone has been sleeping in my bed," roared Papa Bear. "I think someone has been sleeping in my bed," added Mama Bear. "Sleeping in my bed," Baby Bear cried, "and there she is!"

Goldilocks woke up and stared into six furry eyes. "Help!" she screamed as she ran down the stairs and out the front door before the bears could say anything. Home she ran, promising herself that she'd never go into a stranger's house again.

Papa Bear went into his workshop to make Baby Bear a new chair, thinking that this would be a morning he would long remember. Mama went into the kitchen to make some fresh porridge, thinking this had been a most interesting morning. Baby Bear looked through the basket that Goldilocks had left. Finding some muffins and honey in it, he thought that this had been a most interesting morning indeed.

128

Cinderella

Once upon a time, Cinderella, a young girl with a dirty face, sat warming herself next to the fireplace. "I wonder if my stepmother will allow me to go to the ball," she said aloud. "Don't be silly, Cinderella," came an unpleasant voice behind her. It was her stepsister Brunhilde. Her other stepsister, Sassafras, stood next to Brunhilde and yelled, "I would be too embarrassed to be seen with a dirty thing like you." "But," Cinderella said sweetly, "all of the young ladies in the kingdom have been invited." "Well," screamed Brunhilde, "we shall see what Mother has to say about that!" "Yes," echoed Sassafras, "we shall see what mother has to say about that!" And the two hurried out of the kitchen and up the stairs to their mother.

Cinderella began scrubbing the hard stone floor in the kitchen, dreaming about the handsome prince and the ball. Soon she heard footsteps coming toward her. Her cruel stepmother and stepsisters entered. "Cinderella," her stepmother sneered, "Brunhilde and Sassafras tell me you expect to accompany us to the ball. Forget it, my dear. You have entirely too much work to do, and besides, you have nothing to wear." Brunhilde yelled, "Too much work to do!" Sassafras screamed, "Nothing to wear!" And the three turned and walked out of the kitchen.

The night of the ball arrived. Cinderella helped her stepmother and stepsisters dress. After they left, she sat alone by the fire. "How I wanted to go to the ball," she sighed. From the garden came a strange but friendly voice, "And you shall, my dear. You will be the most beautiful lady at the ball." Cinderella hurried out the door and there stood a small old woman with a kindly face holding a large stick. "Who are you?" asked Cinderella. "I'm your fairy godmother, here to get you ready for the ball." With a few quick shakes of her magic wand, Cinderella's rags changed into a beautiful dress and tiny glass slippers appeared on her bare feet. A few more shakes of the wand and a pumpkin and some mice were changed into a horse-drawn carriage. Cinderella's fairy godmother warned, "Be home by midnight for that is when the spell is broken." Then Cinderella rushed off to the ball.

Fairy Tale Party *(cont.)*

Cinderella *(cont.)*

The ball was all that Cinderella had hoped for. The prince danced the entire night with her, ignoring all the other ladies, including Brunhilde and Sassafras. As Cinderella and the prince danced, he would ask, "Who are you? Where did you come from? Why haven't I ever seen you before?" Cinderella would only smile, and her beauty and sweetness would soon make the prince forget he had asked any questions. Cinderella, too, was having a wonderful time, and she forgot to look at the clock. Before she realized it, the bells in the tower were striking twelve, and she began running out of the palace. "Where are you going?" shouted the prince, but Cinderella disappeared. The only thing the prince found was one of her glass slippers, which had fallen off on the steps.

A few days later, the stepsisters were sitting in the kitchen complaining about the ball. "The Prince never even looked at me," cried Brunhilde. "He looked at me," sighed Sassafras, "but only until that strange girl appeared. Then he didn't look at anyone else." The stepmother entered. "Where is Cinderella? I need her to wash the clothes, scrub the steps, and clean the hen house." Brunhilde said, "She's in her room. Ever since we came home from the ball, she's been in some sort of a dream world." "Yes," agreed Sassafras, "she's in a dream world. I couldn't even get her to make my breakfast this morning. The way she's acting, you'd think she had been to the ball and met the prince herself."

At that moment, as if by magic, the prince appeared at their front door. He announced, "I am here to find the girl I danced with at the ball. I have searched almost all the houses in our kingdom looking for the girl whose foot fits in this tiny glass slipper." With that he carefully took the slipper out of his pocket.

Cinderella (cont.)

"May I come in so each of you can try on the slipper?" he asked Brunhilde and Sassafras. The two girls stood there unable to talk. The stepmother caught her breath and invited the prince in. "Come in, your Royal Highness. I am sure the slipper will fit one of my beautiful daughters." As the prince entered the house, he tried to hide his smile at hearing the word "beautiful" to describe these women.

Brunhilde was first, but the slipper would not even go over her toes. "I can't understand it," she screamed, "for this is my slipper — the one I lost the night of the ball!" Then it was Sassafras's turn. It got over her toes, but her heel was sticking out at least three inches from the back. "I think if you push just a bit," she yelled at the prince, "my foot should fit. After all it is my slipper!"

The prince stood up and asked the stepmother, "Are there any other young ladies in this house?" "No," the mother replied, "no other ladies, just the maid we keep to do our work." At that moment, as if by magic, Cinderella appeared in the doorway. "May I try on the slipper?" she asked. The prince, charmed by her sweet voice, replied, "Of course." And, of course, the slipper easily fit Cinderella's foot, for the slipper was indeed hers. Her stepmother screeched and ran from the room.

This time the Prince's smile was not hidden as he picked up Cinderella, put her on his horse, and rode away to the castle with her. Brunhilde screamed, "It's not fair. I wanted to marry the prince." Sassafras yelled, "Cinderella always gets everything she wants. And I hate my big feet!"

Fairy Tale Party *(cont.)*

Clip Art

Baby Bear

Mama Bear

Papa Bear

Goldilocks

Fairy Tale Party (cont.)

Clip Art (cont.)

Castle

Cinderella

Prince

#2510 Party Time

Dinosaur Party

These prehistoric animals are as popular as ever. Announce this party theme, and the guests will come stomping over.

Invitations

Enlarge one of the dinosaurs (pages 138 and 139) so it fills an 8½" x 11" (22 cm x 28 cm) sheet of paper. Write the party information (page 8) on the dinosaur. Mail these invitations in large envelopes with extra postage. This will let the guests know that they are in for a dinosaur party before they even arrive.

Favors and Prizes

Little plastic dinosaurs are a big hit. There are many available for different prices. Make the table an inviting place by putting plastic dinosaurs at each place setting. There are also lots of dinosaur stickers that make nifty favors and prizes.

Table Settings and Decorations

First reproduce several of the dinosaurs (pages 138 and 139) onto stiff paper. Depending on the children's ages and your time, you may need to pre-cut these pictures. When the guests arrive, have them create a mural of "dinosaur land" by drawing mountains, a lake, trees, and plants on a large piece of butcher paper. If you are really brave, you can tape the paper low enough on the wall that the children can color it there. If not, tape it to the floor before they color it. Then, once the scenery is done or the children have had enough, move the mural to the wall. Let the youngsters color some of the dinosaurs. Tape the dinosaurs to the mural. This not only makes a great decoration, it also serves as a backdrop for photographs.

Refreshments

What did dinosaurs eat? Some ate meat; others ate plants. If you decide to have sandwiches, serve some with red meat such as roast beef. You can also serve a platter of vegetables and dip. Otherwise serve traditional party fare.

Dinosaur Party (cont.)

Schedule

15–20 minutes	Children arrive. Look for eggs.
10–15 minutes	Follow the footprints in the sand.
10–15 minutes	Play Dinosaur Tag.
15–20 minutes	Serve refreshments.
10–15 minutes	Open gifts.
10–15 minutes	Play How Big Is a Dinosaur, Really?

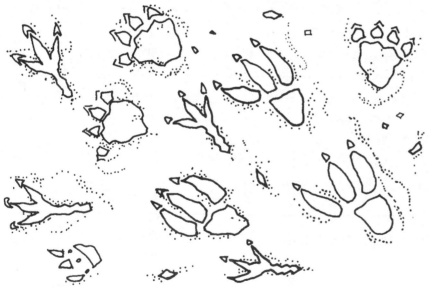

Special

While your child may know all about dinosaurs, there is a chance that you don't. To gather information about these huge creatures, see the chart on page 137.

Activities, Games, and Crafts

Who Am I?

Let your child and the guests share their knowledge about dinosaurs. Find pictures of dinosaurs or use the clip art on pages 138 and 139. Hold up the dinosaur pictures and let the children take turns identifying them. Some children will not only be able to name the creatures, but they will also be able to tell you all kinds of facts.

Looking for Eggs

A fun time can be had by all when you go on a dinosaur egg hunt. You can find plastic Easter eggs — the multicolored kind that separate in half and can be filled — all year round. There are many small dinosaur-related items, such as dinosaur-shaped candy, tiny dinosaur figures, and dinosaur stickers, which you can use to fill up the eggs. To determine how many eggs to hide, decide how many you want each child to find and multiply that by the number of guests. Place the filled eggs around the backyard or in the house. Before the hunt, tell the children how many eggs they can find. Designate a place for them to meet after they find their quota.

Dinosaur Party *(cont.)*

Activities, Games, and Crafts *(cont.)*

Footprints in the Sand

Make dinosaur footprints using construction paper. Place these footprints all over the house with paths that cross and some that lead to nowhere. You will want at least 6–10 different paths. Use different colors for each group of children. Explain to the children that somewhere at the end of the path there is a dinosaur. Let the children work in groups of two or three. If you don't mind them opening doors or drawers, you can make some tracks stop there. For these places, it's a good idea to leave a sign that says something like "Oops, no dino here. Try again." Even if the children find a dinosaur, they should try another path since there may be more than one. The only rule for this hunt is that children have to stay on a path. Doing this outside is a fun-filled activity for little ones. Make sure you have a dinosaur at the end of one path. If you have a different colored path for each group make sure you have a dinosaur at the end of each path.

Dinosaur Tag

Playing tag with a dinosaur twist keeps children moving. The birthday child is "it" first and calls out what type of dinosaur he/she is. Then this child chases the other children, trying to tag another child. The tagged child calls out what kind of dinosaur he/she is and play continues. As a variation, let the children move like dinosaurs, slow and lumbering so they're not always running. It is good to mark boundaries for a game of tag so the children don't go too far. You can always use masking tape to mark the play area for the children.

How Big Is a Dinosaur, Really?

Children are often fascinated by the size of these creatures. Tell them the name of a dinosaur. Ask them to guess how big this dinosaur really was. See the chart on page 137 for this information. Give the children balls of string or yarn. In groups of two, have one hold the string/yarn and the other walk while unraveling it. Have the pair stop when they think that is how big that dinosaur was. Then use a tape measure to determine the length or cut the yarn and measure it. The pair who comes closest are the winners. Give them gummy dinosaurs or candy dino eggs.

Dinosaur Party *(cont.)*

Dinosaur Chart

Name	Nickname	Eater	Size	Notes
Tyrannosaurus	"Tyrant King"	meat eater	20' tall, 53' long	7-inch (18cm) razor-sharp teeth; largest brain; small hands; short neck to support large head
Apatosaurus	"Thunder Lizard"	plant eater	70' tall	spent time in water for balance; feet rounded like an elephant's
Stegosaurus	"Armored Lizard"	plant eater	8' tall, 30' long	double row of plates on back; spiked tail; walnut-sized brain
Diplodocus	"Double Beam"	plant eater	90' long	leathery skin; narrow feet; tail and crane-like neck used for balance
Ankylosaurus	"Curved Lizard"	plant eater	15' long	armored body; clubbed tail; spikes
Pteranodon	"Toothless Wing"	fish eater	25' wing span	largest gliding reptile; may have had light-colored, sun-reflecting fur covering on body
Allosaurus	"Leaping Lizard"	meat eater	36' long	rows of sharp, saw-like teeth; walked on hind legs
Brachiosaurus	"Arm Lizard"	plant eater	75' long, 39' tall	heaviest animal ever; small brain; pillar-like front legs were longer than back legs
Ichthyosaurus	"Fish Lizard"	plant eater	10–30' long	dolphin-like marine reptile; once lived on land, adapted to water; very fast swimmer
Dimetrodon	"Double Measure Tooth"	meat eater	9' long	early reptile; large spiked fin on back (used to adjust body heat)
Parasaurolophus	"Duck Billed"	plant eater	30' long	duck billed, webbed feet; 2,000 teeth for grinding food
Iguanadon	"Iguana Tooth"	plant eater	18' tall, 30' long	used tail for balance; horned thumbs; could walk on two or four feet
Protoceratops	"First-Horned Face"	plant eater	3' tall, 6' long	size of a large dog; nose ended in parrot-like beak; large, bony frill at the back of the head
Triceratops	"Three-Horned Face"	plant eater	6' tall, 25' long	protected by armor, used horns in fight; very short, strong neck

Dinosaur Party (cont.)

Clip Art

Dimetrodon

Apatosaurus

Pteranodon

Stegosaurus

Dinosaur Party *(cont.)*

Clip Art *(cont.)*

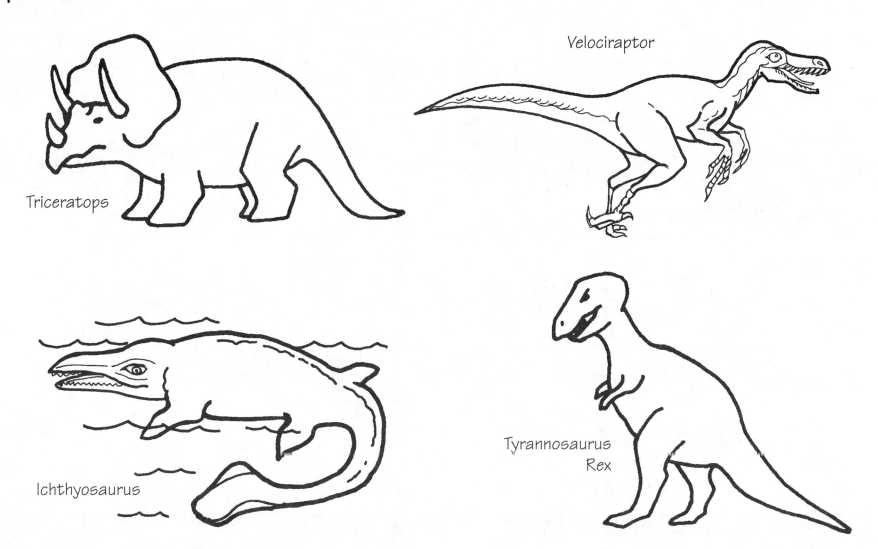

Triceratops

Velociraptor

Ichthyosaurus

Tyrannosaurus Rex

A Backward, Inside Out Party

Start at the very end, go to the middle, and end at the very beginning!

Invitations

Create the invitation for this party by putting everything on it backwards. For example, write the ending time first and then the starting time. Make sure the parents understand this so that they don't bring their child at the end of the party.

Table Settings and Decorations

Set the table backwards. Turn the tablecloth inside out, place the forks, knives, spoons, plates, and glasses upside down. Hang any pictures, posters, or decorations upside down. Write the children's names backwards on the place cards.

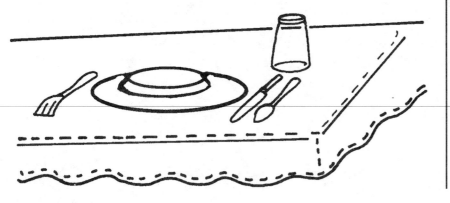

Refreshments

Serve the food for this party in the opposite order than you might normally do so. Bring out the ice cream first, then the drinks, and finally the cake. If you are making a meal, serve it after dessert.

However, be prepared for children not to eat it! For a special birthday cake, serve a pineapple upside-down cake.

Schedule

15–25 minutes	Children arrive. Decorate "Eman."
15–20 minutes	Serve refreshments.
10–15 minutes	Open gifts.
20–30 minutes	Do Backwards Races and the Get Dressed Backwards contest.
10–15 minutes	Play Backwards Words.

Special

Have children come to the party with their clothes on backwards or inside out. (**Warning:** Don't let them wear shoes backwards since this can be dangerous.) Instead of greeting children at the front door, have them come in the back door. Put out a sign that reads EMOCLEW OT YM YTRAP (page 142).

A Backward, Inside Out Party *(cont.)*

Activities, Games, and Crafts

Backwards Races

Have the children stand at the starting line. When you say "Go," have them walk backwards to the finish line.

Get Dressed Backwards

Play this twist on the getting dressed game. Have two suitcases full of old, oversized clothes. Usually a pair of pants, a shirt, a jacket, a pair of shoes, and a hat are plenty. Place the same amount of clothes in each suitcase. Put the children into two teams. Have one child from each team put on all the clothes. When you say "Go," they take the clothes off, place them in the suitcase, and the next child puts on the clothes. The team that takes all the suitcase clothes off first is the winner. A variation of this is to have the children put these clothes on backwards.

Backward Words

Depending on the age of the children, you can do this game by writing words or saying them aloud. Write a list of easy words, both forward and backward. Then read a word backward to the children, or if you're writing it for them, put it on poster board so all of them can see it. Say the word aloud and see if the children recognize it. (**Note:** Practice the words before you say them aloud. If children are having trouble guessing, give them clues, such as the first letter of the word or a definition for it.) For beginning readers, choose easy words like *cat*, which becomes *tac*. Remember this is all in fun, so if the children don't get a word, tell it to them.

Decorate Your Eman

What is an *Eman*? Why, it's a name spelled backwards. Prepare a placemat or name card for each child by writing her/his name backwards on it. Use a computer or create stencil letters that can be filled in. Provide crayons, markers, or colored pens and have the children decorate these and place them at the table.

Clip Art

EMOCLEW OT

YM YTRAP

Be a Star! Party

If you have a child who is sure she or he is Hollywood bound, this is just the party for this youngster!

Invitations

Send out invitations that feature a huge star in the middle. Use the star on page 147 with the words "Be a Star!" in the middle. Then write the rest of the invitation (page 8) on the points of the star. Star confetti is usually available at stationery stores and is fun to include in the invitation. Be sure you do not use too much.

Favors and Prizes

Sunglasses make great favors and prizes for children. See Activities, Games, and Crafts (page 145) for making them even more fun.

Table Settings and Decorations

Use the Star Chains (page 34) to help decorate for this party. Roll out the red carpet for the children to use when they enter. You can do this by unwrapping a roll of red wrapping paper or red plastic table covering sold by the foot at party stores. Just make sure to tape it down.

Use star confetti to help decorate the table. The cake can feature a photo of the birthday child. To do this simply, use a craft stick and glue a picture of the birthday star onto it. You can use construction paper strips to frame it and place it in the middle of the cake. As an alternative, you can use the star on page 147 and glue the child's picture on it. Then glue the star onto a craft stick.

Refreshments

Star-shaped cookie cutters can be pressed into service to create sandwiches or cookies in this shape. Cookies can be frosted with silver icing or decorated with edible silver decorations. Sparkling juice can be served. There are many on the market, or you can add lemon-lime soda to clear juice for the same effect.

Schedule

15–20 minutes	Children arrive. Make sunglasses.
15–20 minutes	Dress like a star.
20–30 minutes	Do the Lip-Sync or Pint-Size Karaoke.
15–20 minutes	Serve refreshments.
10–15 minutes	Open gifts.
15–20 minutes	Make Movie Star Collages.

Special

If you decide to videotape any of the activities, encourage parents to come for a quick screening at the end of the party. If you want to add to the laughter, show the video backwards!

You might also want to give awards, such as the Oscars, to all the children. These can be small trophies or ribbons. See page 147 for a ribbon pattern that you can reproduce and use for this purpose.

144

Be a Star! Party *(cont.)*

Activities, Games, and Crafts

Decorating Sunglasses

Provide each child with an inexpensive pair of sunglasses. (**Note:** Tell parents that these sunglasses are for fun, not sun protection.) Let the children glue glitter, feathers, and sequins, onto their sunglasses as decorations. Let the glue dry before the children put them on.

Dress Like a Star

Provide a box of old fancy clothing. Thrift shops or cleaned out closets may provide all the things you need. Put in as many fancy type things as you can. Clothing items might include hats, gloves, boas, ties, shoes, tuxedo shirts or jackets, purses, and capes. A good dose of costume jewelry can also be added to the collection. Let the children have a chance to dress up and show off the outfits they have created. As an option, you can have the children come dressed in clothing that they feel befits a star.

Be a Star! Party (cont.)

Activities, Games, and Crafts (cont.)

Lip Sync

Find some music that children are familiar with. Check with the birthday child well before the party to pick the music. There might be a children's performer or a song that is popular with the young set that you already have in your collection of tapes or CDs. Let the children practice some lip syncing. You may wish to have them do this after they have dressed up like stars (page 145). Then when they seem ready to perform, videotape them. Remember, the object is not to go for perfection or even close to that. It is simply to have fun.

Pint-Size Karaoke

Real Karaoke has the words displayed on a screen as the performer sings along. Create your own version of this by providing a microphone and a tape recorder with some very familiar sing-along tapes. Let children take turns singing into the microphone. If they want to sing in groups, that is fine. Again, this is a great opportunity to videotape them.

Movie Star Collages

To make these collages, you will need to collect pictures of actors and actresses you think your child and the guests will recognize. Start a few weeks in advance of the party. Scour magazines, newspapers, and Web sites. Clip the pictures out and let the children make collages by gluing the pictures onto 8 ½" x 11" (22 cm x 28 cm) sheets of stiff paper. Let them decorate their collages with glitter.

Dancing

Little children love to dance. Put on some music and let the children dance to the beat. This will be worth capturing on film. It will be even more enjoyable if they wear their star clothes.

Clip Art

Star

Be a Star!

Ribbon

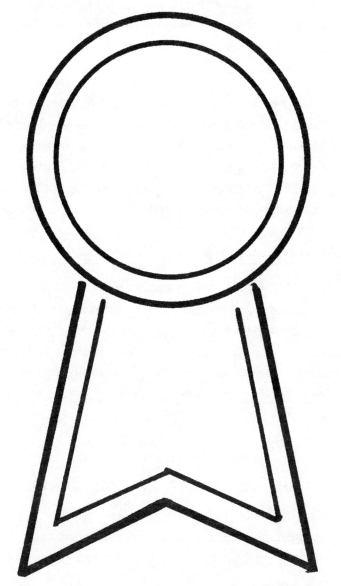

Teddy Bears' Picnic

Let little ones bring their teddy bears to celebrate the birthday child.

Invitations

Use the clip art on page 151 to create an invitation. Reproduce it and glue it onto a large piece of paper. Make sure to include all the party information (page 8), emphasizing that each guest should bring a teddy bear or other stuffed animal. (**Note:** You might want to keep a few extra on hand in case some guests forget.)

Favors and Prizes

Anything that has a teddy bear, such as stickers and notepaper, will make a wonderful favor or prize. Little teddy bear figurines or small stuffed teddies will also work. You can wrap the teddy bears up in large red and white checkered napkins that are found at many grocery stores. Picnic items, such as plastic cups with the guests' names written on them, make more nice favors. They can also use these cups during the party.

Table Settings and Decorations

This party can be held at a regular table, a picnic table, or on the ground with a blanket or old tablecloth spread out for the children to sit on. A checked tablecloth or napkins often help add to the atmosphere. Seat the children's teddy bears at the table as decorations. For each teddy bear, provide a large paper plate that says, "This space is reserved for _____ 's teddy bear." Write a child's name in the blank. Encourage the children to leave their teddies in the reserved seats whenever they are not playing with them. If you are using a blanket or tablecloth on the ground, line up the reserved seats plates in a row and tape them down.

A teddy bear birthday cake is always a big hit. If making your own, you can often find bear-shaped pans in the baking sections of cooking, department, and craft stores.

148

Refreshments

A picnic with finger foods is just the ticket for this party. Peanut butter and jelly sandwiches with chips or carrots, juice, and bear-shaped cookies are plenty for little appetites. Pack a picnic basket for effect and serve out of it, or give each child a paper sack with his/her name and Teddy bear stickers on it.

Schedule

15–20 minutes	Children arrive. Make teddy bear hats.
20–25 minutes	Take pictures in the woods.
15–20 minutes	Drop the spoons in the honey pot.
15–20 minutes	Serve refreshments.
10–15 minutes	Open gifts.
20–30 minutes	Make Teddy Beddys.

Special

This party can be held outdoors in a backyard or park on a warm sunny day or indoors with a blanket spread on the floor on a cold, blustery day.

Activities, Games, and Crafts

Goldilocks and the Three Bears

See the Fairy Tale Party (pages 127 and 128) for a version of this story. Have children create the puppets (page 132), or just read the story aloud to them.

Teddy Bear Hats

Use the pattern (page 151) to create the hats. Depending on the age of the children, you may need to pre-cut the teddy bears. If they are old enough, let them color and cut the teddy bears. Provide crayons and markers. As the children finish coloring their teddy bears, help them staple or tape the bears to long strips of construction paper to create the headbands. Invite the children to wear their teddy bear hats.

Activities, Games, and Crafts *(cont.)*

A Picture in the Woods

Before the party, draw a teddy bear in an outdoor setting on butcher paper that is 7 feet (2.m) long. Make the teddy big enough so that a child's face can replace the teddy bear's face. Cut a hole where the teddy bear's face should be. Color the drawing. Hang the butcher paper from a clothesline or attach it to pieces of cardboard that are taped together. Make sure the teddy's face is less than 3 feet (0.9 m) off the ground. Take pictures of the children sticking their faces through the hole. As a variation, draw more teddies. (**Note:** Don't be intimidated by the art required for this project. The teddy bear can be a simple outline drawing and the woods can be triangular trees. The party guests can even help make the drawing.)

Drop the Spoons in the Honey Pot

Bears love to eat honey. Get a large pot and label it with the word "honey." The children can stand behind a chair or kneel facing the back of a chair. Then have them take turns dropping 10 plastic spoons into the honey pot. This way they have to drop the spoons over the chair, which presents more of a challenge.

Teddy Beddys

Once you know how many guests you are having at the party, you can determine how many shoe boxes you will need to collect. Try to use adult-sized shoe boxes. Have some larger boxes since some teddy bears are quite big. Let the children create beds for their teddy bears. Provide wrapping paper, fabric scraps, rickrack, stuffing, construction paper, scissors (that cut different designs), various types and colors of paper, tape, and any other decorating materials you have available. Let each child be as creative as possible. This is a good activity for the children to do when they get to the party. Prepare a work area, and have the materials ready for them. Help the children choose boxes that are the right size for their bears. Show them how to use scissors with various decorative edges to create blankets and pillows. Make sure the children don't put a teddy in its bed if the glue isn't dry.

Clip Art

Teddy Bear

Honey Pot

House Camping Party

If you have a young camper in your house, this party will be a winner — especially if Mom and Dad prefer a hotel when on vacation.

Invitations

Make an invitation using the picture of a tent shown below. You can enlarge and reproduce the tent. Then glue it onto the top half of a piece of paper. Write the party information (page 8) on the bottom half of the paper.

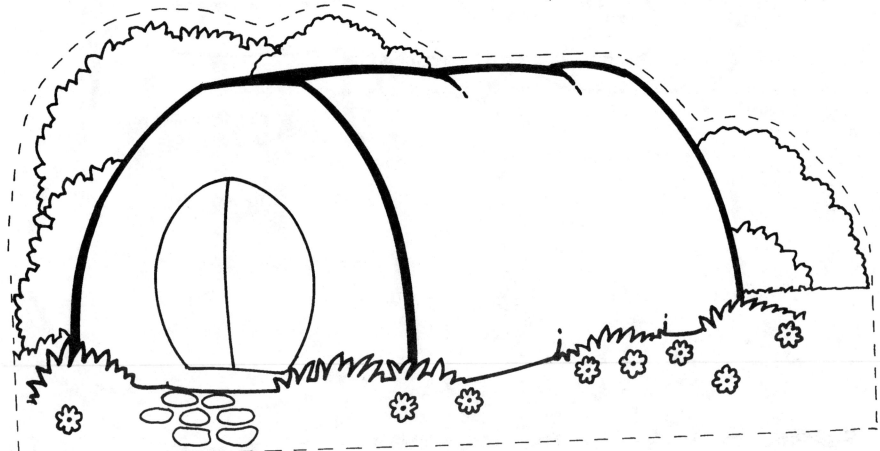

House Camping Party *(cont.)*

Favors and Prizes

Camping items, such as waterproof pouches, zipper bags, combs, freeze-dried treats, boxes of raisins, whistles, compasses, or small flashlights will be welcomed. Stickers with trees or flowers on them are also fun for children to receive.

Table Settings and Decorations

If your family has camping equipment, set up a tent or open some sleeping bags for the children to sit on. For the cake, you can make a forest scene using plastic miniature trees and forest animals. Otherwise, you can put some candles into a few of the marshmallows used for the s'mores and make this the birthday cake.

Refreshments

Campers can prepare their own food to be eaten later in the party. Pizza bagels, cheese and crackers, and other finger foods can all be served with hot chocolate or lemonade. Make the classic camp treats — s'mores for dessert.

Schedule

20–25 minutes	Children arrive. Pitch tents.
15–20 minutes	Prepare camp food.
20–25 minutes	Play games.
15–20 minutes	Eat and make s'mores.
20–30 minutes	Go in tents for present opening, Scary Stories, and Silly Time.

Activities, Games, and Crafts

Pitching Tents

Help the children make their own tents by draping sheets and blankets over chairs that are placed at even intervals around a room. You may need to tie a sheet between every two chairs to help support the tents. The children will be delighted with the colorful tent city they have made.

House Camping Party (cont.)

Activities, Games, and Crafts (cont.)

Make the Camp Food

Pizza bagels are a hit. However, if you don't want to deal with food falling through the hole, use English muffins instead. Slice the bread in half before you let the partygoers into the kitchen. Set out pizza fixings, such as grated cheese, pepperoni, and tomatoes or tomato sauce. Heat the pizzas later. In addition, you can have the children prepare crackers with toppings and roll pastry around miniature hot dogs. Like the pizzas, heat the hot dogs later.

Neighborhood Hike — Follow the Leader

Your child can be the leader and escort the party guests around the neighborhood. Keep the children in a single file line and have the leader take a fun circuitous route through the schoolyard or park. It will be especially entertaining if you can include some playground equipment along the route. You may wish to let the children take turns being the leader. Do this only around your neighborhood. If there is no park, see if you can entice a couple of neighbors to let your campers go into their yards or houses. The children will think this is hilarious, and any neighbor that would let you tramp through will enjoy this too.

Let's Eat

Campers get mighty hungry, so you'd better feed them. Heat up those pizzas and serve them with the other foods that the campers made. You can let them eat in the tents they have pitched in a kid-safe campground. If the ground is actually your carpet, you may prefer to set up a table with an outdoor tablecloth. Use paper plates and plastic utensils. Here's one party where you don't have to spend much on the table settings. The dessert will require major thought. It can be dangerous to roast marshmallows over the stove or fireplace — although it can be done. A safer suggestion is s'mores, using the microwave to soften the marshmallows.

Activities, Games, and Crafts *(cont.)*

Craft Stick Building

Do some activities that one might do at camp. Provide lots of craft sticks and white glue. Have the children make boxes with them. These are pretty simple to create, and you and your child might want to make one before the party to use as a model. Take 10 to 20 craft sticks and glue them side-by-side to create the bottom. Then begin the sides by gluing a stick on either side of the bottom. Next glue two more in the opposite direction. Continue to do this until you get to the top or as high as you want the box to be. You can create a top just like the bottom, but be sure you don't glue it onto the box.

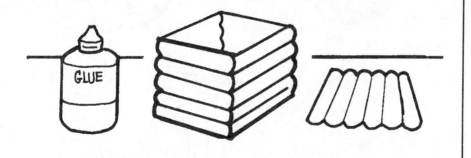

Opening Presents

It is time to climb into the tent. Have your child open presents under the sheets and blankets. Take lots of pictures since it might just be a once in a lifetime experience.

Scary Stories

What would a camp out be without ghost stories? Decide with your child how frightening you want these to be. If your youngster likes scary stories, try to get the room as dark as possible and use a flashlight to read the stories. Add sound effects.

Silly Time

Give the children a few minutes at the end of the party to enjoy the tent. You don't have to plan anything. Leave them to their own imaginations. The only problem will probably be getting them to come out when their parents come to pick them up.

Backyard Bash

If your child and friends are into games, this might be a birthday party that allows them to use their youthful energy — and keeps them out of the house.

Invitations

Use the clip art of the fence shown below as the outside of the invitation. Reproduce it and write the invitation information (page 8) on the inside.

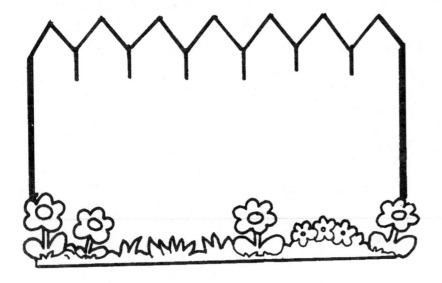

Favors and Prizes

Since there are so many games at this party, you'll want to seriously consider the sort of prizes you give. One alternative to prizes is to make medals, using gold seals or ribbons (Use the pattern on page 147.) This will certainly keep the cost down, and no one athlete will leave the bash with half of the cost of the party.

Favors could be pamphlets or books about sports teams or the Olympic games, sports stickers, jumpropes, Chinese jumpropes, or key chains that dangle a soccer ball or basketball.

 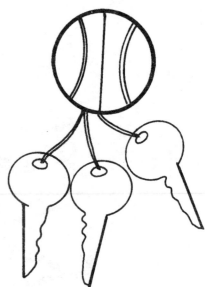

Backyard Bash (cont.)

Table Settings and Decorations

Prepare two tables, one for the food and one for sitting. If you cannot find any sports-related tableware, you can use the colors of your child's favorite sport team — one color for the tablecloth and the other color for the plates and cups. Place some sports equipment down the center, and you'll have a winner of a table.

Refreshments

If you are serving food, hamburgers and hot dogs would be the obvious choice for this party. Set up a food line on one table and seat the children at another. This will allow them to have fun preparing their plates, while keeping the mess away from where they are sitting. It should be much easier to supervise this way. All you'll probably need to do is refill their drink cups and offer a few more potato chips.

Schedule

10–20 minutes	Children arrive. Play Name Game or Taking a Trip Game.
20–30 minutes	Choose teams and have several relays.
15–20 minutes	Serve refreshments.
10–20 minutes	Open gifts.
10–20 minutes	Play quiet games.

Special

If you have a friend who is a coach or on a sports team, invite this person to the party to talk for a few minutes about his/her team. Ask this speaker to stress the importance of teamwork before the children play the party games. This might keep the more boisterous youngsters from getting out of control. Of course, the idea of teamwork is an important concept to reinforce with children. Hearing it from an adult or an older child involved in sports is an excellent addition to this party.

Backyard Bash *(cont.)*

Activities, Games, and Crafts

Since this party will consist mainly of games, you should ask your child to help you choose the ones that the guests will play. However, pick games that are mostly relays rather than a soccer or football game.

Choosing Teams

We suggest that an adult help with this part. You want to make sure that no one feels left out. You might simply have each child pick an envelope out of a dish. Prepare the envelopes ahead of time by putting a green or red paper square in each. Those with a green square form one team, while those with a red square form the other. You might have your child change teams for different relays if she/he is old enough to understand this concept. If not, have your child also choose an envelope.

Shoe Box Relay

Divide the group into two teams. Give each team two shoeboxes that are large enough to be worn by the child who has the largest feet. Line up the teams. The first player puts the shoeboxes on her/his feet and shuffles to a specific point and back again. That player takes off the shoeboxes and gives them to the next person in line. Then the new player shuffles across the floor wearing the shoeboxes. The first team to have each member do the shuffle, wins.

Basketball Relay

Two teams line up in single file. The first player on each team is given a basketball or soccer ball. That player passes it over her/his head to the next player. The second player passes the ball between her/his legs to the third player, and so on. When the person on the end gets the ball, she/he runs to the front of the line and the passing begins again. The first team to get back in the original order wins.

Backyard Bash (cont.)

Activities, Games, and Crafts (cont.)

Spoon-and-Egg Relay

Give each player a spoon. Place about a dozen eggs on a table in front of the two teams. Have the players spread out at least a double arm's length from one another. The first player runs to the table, puts an egg on the spoon, and, as quickly as possible, goes to the second player and transfers the egg without using his/her hands. The egg is passed down the line. The first team to pass the egg down the line without breaking it, wins. If a child drops the egg and it breaks, he/she must return to the table, get a new egg, and give it to the next player. A variation is to pass four or five eggs down the line — the first player would get a new egg as soon as the first one is passed to another player. (**Note:** You might think about using hard boiled eggs, golf balls, or marbles for less of a mess.)

Pick-Up-One-More Relay

Collect 6–10 identical pairs of objects, such as two balls, two plastic cups, two crayons, and two books. Set up two tables and place one of each item on each table. Line up two teams. The first player on each team runs to the table, grabs an item, and gives it to the second player. The second player must take that item, run to the table, and locate the identical object. The second player grabs the identical item and a third item. That player takes the three objects to the third player. Play continues in this manner. The winning team is the one whose last player is able to hang on to all the paired items while returning to his/her place in line. The first player should return any item that is dropped to the table.

Backyard Bash (cont.)

Activities, Games, and Crafts (cont.)

Wet-Head-and-Balloon-Waddle Relay

This will get them wet, but it is so much fun that most children will love it. Each team member must walk to a specified point with a balloon held between his/her knees and a cup of water balanced on his/her head. If either the balloon breaks or the cup falls, the player starts over. Set up two tables with several balloons and cups that are half filled with water. The first player goes to the table, puts a balloon between his/her knees and a cup on his/her head, goes to the specified location, then returns the balloon and cup to the table. Then this player tags the next person in line, and so on. If a cup falls or a balloon breaks as a player is returning them to the table, there is no foul.

You might need to place a mark a couple of feet from the table to show that this is where they can remove the cups from their heads and the balloons from between their knees. (**Note:** You might have your child try a few different kinds of cups to find the one that is easiest to balance.)

Other Relays

Don't dismiss those old favorites, such as the sack race and the three-legged race, as well as any of your child's favorites.

Keeping Score

You need to decide ahead of time if you will keep track of the points that the teams earn. If you do, you might keep a running total on a poster board so that the teams can see how they are doing. Give certificates or small prizes to the winners.